The Debt Freedom System

The Exact Order to Pay Off What You Owe

Daniel Cross

First edition, 2026

Published by Daniel Cross

This book is intended for general educational and reflective purposes only. It is not a substitute for professional financial, legal, medical, or mental health advice, diagnosis, or treatment. Always seek the advice of a qualified professional with any questions regarding your specific circumstances. Never disregard professional advice or delay seeking it because of something you have read in this book. Names and identifying details in any illustrative examples are anonymous/archetypal composites, not depictions of a single real individual.

Contents

Foreword

I spent four years underwriting consumer loans before I ever wrote a word about money. Every file that crossed my desk told the same story from a different angle: a person who was not stupid, not reckless, not bad with money in any way that would show up on a personality test — just carrying debt in an order that made it nearly impossible to win.

That's the thing nobody tells you. The debt itself is rarely the whole problem. The order you attack it in is a separate variable, and it's one almost nobody optimizes, because almost nobody is taught to think of it as a variable at all. You get a bill. You pay what's due. You get another bill. Repeat, for years, while the arithmetic quietly works against you in the background — a 24% card growing faster than a 6% loan you've been throwing extra money at because it has the bigger, scarier balance.

I wrote this book because the fix for that isn't complicated. It isn't a personality overhaul, and it isn't a secret only wealthy people know. It's math you can do on a phone calculator, applied in a specific sequence, combined with a handful of scripts that get creditors to actually negotiate instead of just collect. That's the whole book. No mindset chapter. No workbook about your relationship with money. Just the order, the math behind the order, and what to say to the people you owe.

I want to be honest about one more thing up front, because it matters: this book will not tell you debt is a moral failing you need to atone for. It's a financial position, and financial positions get corrected with financial mechanics. If you're holding this book, you already know you want out. What you may not have is the exact sequence that gets you there fastest, with the least amount of money handed unnecessarily to a bank along the way.

That sequence is what follows.

— Daniel Cross

Introduction

Here's a number worth sitting with before we go any further: paid off in the wrong order, two people with the identical total debt, the identical income, and the identical monthly payment can finish years apart — and one of them can pay thousands of dollars more in interest than the other, for no reason except the sequence they chose. Same debt. Same effort. Different math. That gap is not theoretical. It's arithmetic, and arithmetic doesn't care how motivated you are.

This book exists to close that gap. Not by telling you to want it more, budget harder, or examine why you got into debt in the first place — there's a place for that conversation, and this isn't it. This book exists to hand you the actual mechanics: what your debt really costs you once you strip away the monthly-payment illusion, which payoff order wins in which situation and why, how to negotiate a lower balance with a creditor who has more leverage than you think, when consolidation saves you real money and when it just moves the furniture around a room that's still on fire, and what to do with your life once the debt is gone so you don't find yourself back here in three years.

If you've read any debt book before, you've probably run into two philosophies presented as a religious choice: the debt avalanche (highest interest rate first, mathematically optimal) versus the debt snowball (smallest balance first, psychologically easier to sustain). Most books pick a side and defend it. This book won't, because picking a side is the wrong frame. The honest answer is that both are correct descriptions of different things — one describes which order saves the most money, the other describes which order most people actually finish. You need both pieces of information to build a real plan, and you'll get both, with the actual math laid out so you can run it on your own numbers instead of taking anyone's word for it.

A word about how the numbers in this book are meant to be used before we go any further, because it changes how you should read every chapter ahead. Nothing in this book asks you to trust a claim on faith. Every mechanism described — the true cost of a minimum payment, the avalanche-versus-snowball gap, the break-even math on a balance transfer, the total-cost comparison on a consolidation offer — is something you can independently verify with a calculator and your own real account numbers, in most cases in under fifteen minutes per calculation. That's a deliberate design choice, not an incidental one. A book that asked you to simply believe its conclusions would be asking for something this subject doesn't require and shouldn't get. Run the numbers yourself, on your own debts, as you go — the book will be more useful for it, and so will the plan you build from it.

A word about what this book is not. It is not a book about why you're in debt. It doesn't matter, for the purposes of what follows, whether the balance came from a medical emergency, a business that didn't work out, years of overspending, a divorce, student loans that outpaced your first-decade income, or some combination no single label captures. The mechanics in this book work identically regardless of the story behind the number. If you're looking for a book that helps you understand the psychological pattern that led to debt in the first place — the emotional pull toward spending, the specific reflex that makes a limit feel like a target — that's a real and valuable subject, and it's simply not the subject of this book. This one starts from where you are today: an actual list of actual balances at actual interest rates, and the exact order to attack them.

It's also not a book about budgeting from scratch, building an emergency fund from zero, or increasing your income. Those are real levers, and they matter, but they're general personal-finance mechanics that plenty of other resources already cover well. This book has one job: take whatever amount of money you've already decided to put toward debt each month, and make sure every dollar of it is doing the maximum possible work. That's a narrower, more mechanical promise than most debt books make, and it's one this book can actually keep.

Here's how the book is built. Each chapter follows the same shape: a real situation you'll likely recognize, the mechanics underneath it explained plainly, a concrete script or framework you can use immediately, and a worked example with real numbers so you can see the mechanism operate end to end rather than just take the principle on faith. Chapter 1 establishes what a debt actually costs you, which turns out to be a very different number than the one printed on your statement. Chapters 2 and 3 build your payoff order, using the real avalanche-versus-snowball math and a hybrid method most books never mention. Chapters 4 through 6 cover the three levers most people never pull — negotiating directly with a creditor or collector, consolidation done honestly, and balance transfers done correctly. Chapter 7 addresses the one psychological question this book does tackle directly, because it's tactical rather than diagnostic: which payoff order keeps a person moving long enough to actually finish. Chapter 8 handles the real-world mess of multiple debt types at once — credit cards, student loans, medical bills, and car loans, which don't all follow the same rules. Chapter 9 covers the part almost no debt book addresses seriously: what happens after the last balance hits zero, and how to make sure it stays that way. Chapter 10 closes with the ten mistakes that add the most unnecessary time and money to a payoff plan, gathered from patterns that show up again and again regardless of the specific numbers involved.

One practical note before you start. Go get your real numbers before you read Chapter 1 — every balance, every interest rate, every minimum payment, for every debt you carry. Write them down or pull up your account statements. The book will ask you to run your own math in several places, and estimated numbers produce an estimated plan. Real numbers produce a real one.

A word on the numbers used throughout this book

Every dollar figure, interest rate, and calculated outcome in the chapters ahead is illustrative — chosen to demonstrate a mechanism clearly, not pulled from any specific real account or lender. Interest rates on credit cards, personal loans, and other consumer debt move with broader economic conditions and vary meaningfully by lender, credit profile, and debt type, which means a specific rate quoted as typical in this book may look different from the specific rate on your own statement by the time you're reading this. That variation doesn't undermine anything in the chapters that follow, because what this book actually teaches is never a specific number — it's the logic underneath the number: how to calculate what a given rate and balance actually cost you, how to compare two payoff orders using your own figures, how to evaluate whether a specific consolidation or transfer offer helps or hurts once its full terms are run through the frameworks provided. Plug your own real numbers into these frameworks throughout, rather than assuming the illustrative figures in any worked example describe your situation precisely. The math is the product. The specific numbers are just how the math gets demonstrated.

It's also worth being direct about what this book will not do, because a book that tells you exactly what it won't do is easier to trust on what it will. It will not recommend a specific lender, credit counseling agency, app, or financial product by name — brand-specific recommendations age quickly and this book is built to remain useful regardless of which specific companies exist or which specific offers are on the market when you're reading it. It will not tell you a specific dollar amount you personally should have in an emergency fund, a specific percentage of income you should allocate to debt payoff versus other goals, or a specific timeline you should hit — those are individual decisions that depend on your income, obligations, and risk tolerance, and a book claiming to know the universal right answer to any of them would be overstating what any book can actually know about your specific life. What it will do, consistently, chapter after chapter, is hand you the exact calculation to run so you can answer those questions correctly for yourself, with your own real numbers, rather than guessing or copying someone else's plan wholesale.

Let's start with what your debt is actually costing you, because it's almost certainly not what your statement makes it look like.

Chapter 1 — What Your Debt Actually Costs You

The situation

A monthly credit card statement is, structurally, one of the most quietly misleading documents most people read on a regular basis. Not because it lies — every number on it is technically accurate — but because of what it puts in large type and what it buries. The balance is prominent. The minimum payment is prominent, usually in a box, sometimes with a little "pay this and stay current" reassurance built into the layout. The number that actually determines your financial future — how much this debt will cost you if you keep paying the way you've been paying — is either absent or printed in a sentence most people's eyes slide right past.

Picture someone carrying a balance of $6,000 on a card with an 22% annual interest rate, paying the minimum every month because the minimum is what fits the budget and the balance never seems to move much. That last part isn't a coincidence or a sign they're doing anything unusual — it's the mechanism working exactly as the mechanism is built to work. At a typical minimum-payment formula (roughly 1-2% of the balance plus that month's interest), it can take well over fifteen years to pay off that $6,000 balance, and the total interest paid along the way can exceed the original balance itself. The card gets used for less and less over those years. The balance still barely moves. That's not bad luck. That's the math doing precisely what it was designed to do.

The mechanics

Here is the mechanism, stated plainly: a minimum payment is calculated to keep you paying for as long as possible while satisfying the smallest number the lender is legally allowed to accept. It is not calculated to get you out of debt efficiently, because efficient payoff was never the minimum payment's job. Its job is to keep the account open, keep you current, and keep interest accruing on the remaining balance for as many months as the formula can stretch it.

Three numbers matter far more than your statement makes them look like they matter.

Annual Percentage Rate (APR) is the yearly cost of carrying a balance, expressed as a percentage. But APR by itself tells you less than it looks like it tells you, because most revolving debt (credit cards, most personal lines of credit) compounds — interest is charged not just on your original balance, but on previously accrued interest that never got paid off. A 22% APR compounded daily or monthly behaves meaningfully differently than a simple 22% charged once a year, and it's always worse for you than the headline number suggests. This is why two debts with the same APR but different compounding frequency cost different amounts — always check your card agreement for compounding frequency, not just the rate.

Minimum payment structure typically works out to a percentage of your current balance (commonly 1-3%) plus that period's accrued interest, with a small dollar floor. As your balance shrinks, ever so slightly, the minimum payment shrinks with it — which means the loan never builds real momentum on its own. You are not climbing a fixed staircase where each step gets you measurably closer. You are on a treadmill whose speed adjusts downward exactly in proportion to how far you've walked.

Total interest paid over the life of the debt is the number your statement never prints, and it's the only number that actually tells you what the debt costs you. It requires knowing the balance, the rate, the payment amount, and running an amortization calculation — which is a fancy way of saying "figure out, month by month, how much of each payment goes to interest versus principal, until the balance hits zero." This is the number that determines whether a debt is a minor inconvenience or a five-figure drain on your life, and it is entirely a function of the payment amount and the order you attack multiple debts in — both of which are things you control.

There's a second layer worth understanding, because it explains why some debts feel so much harder to move than others even at similar balances: **the amortization curve**. Early in any loan's life — especially a longer-term installment loan like a mortgage, auto loan, or long-term personal loan — a larger share of each payment goes to interest, and a smaller share reduces the actual principal. As the balance shrinks over time, that ratio flips: more of each payment starts chipping into principal. This is why the first few years of a long loan can feel like you're barely making progress despite years of on-time payments, and why extra payments made early in a loan's life are disproportionately more valuable than the same extra payment made later — an early payment attacks principal at the point where the least of your regular payment is doing that job, which means the interest savings compound over the maximum remaining number of months.

Revolving debt (credit cards, most lines of credit) doesn't amortize the same predictable way installment loans do, because the balance itself can move up or down with new charges. But the underlying principle carries over identically: extra payments made now, while the balance is at its current size, save more total interest than the same extra payment made later, because every dollar of principal you eliminate today stops accruing interest for every remaining day you'd otherwise have carried it.

The framework

Here's a three-step framework for finding out what a debt actually costs you, usable on any balance with a calculator or a basic spreadsheet.

Step one: find your real APR. Not the promotional rate, not the rate you remember signing up for — the current rate on your most recent statement or account portal. Rates on variable-rate cards and lines of credit move with broader interest-rate cycles; check the actual current number, not an old one from memory.

Step two: calculate total interest at your current payment. Most bank account portals and credit card issuer apps now include an interest calculator or "payoff estimate" feature that will show you, using your real numbers, how long a balance takes to clear and how much interest you'll pay along the way at your current payment level. If yours doesn't, any basic loan-amortization calculator (widely and freely available, and you don't need a specific named tool — any standard one that takes balance, rate, and payment will do) gets you the same answer. Plug in your balance, your APR, and your current monthly payment.

Step three: calculate total interest at a higher payment. Run the same calculation again, this time adding some fixed amount — $50, $100, whatever's realistic — to your monthly payment. Compare the two total-interest numbers and the two payoff-time numbers side by side. This comparison is the single most motivating piece of math in personal finance, because it converts an abstract sense of "I should pay more" into a concrete, specific dollar figure and month count that a slightly larger payment actually buys you.

The worked example

Take that $6,000 balance at 22% APR. At a minimum payment that starts around $180 and shrinks as the balance shrinks, that debt can take over 15 years to clear and cost more than $6,000 in interest alone — meaning the true cost of that debt, principal plus interest, runs close to double the original balance.

Now run the same $6,000 at 22% APR with a fixed $250 monthly payment instead of a shrinking minimum. The payoff time drops to roughly 28-29 months — a little over two years, instead of over fifteen — and total interest paid drops to somewhere in the neighborhood of $1,300-$1,500, instead of exceeding $6,000. Same debt. Same interest rate. A payment increase of roughly $70-100 over what the minimum would have started at, held fixed instead of shrinking, is the entire difference between a fifteen-year sentence and a two-year one, and between paying more than double the original balance in interest versus paying about a fifth of it.

That gap — thirteen years and roughly $4,500-5,000 in interest — is not a rounding error. It's the actual, dollar-for-dollar cost of not knowing this math, multiplied across however many debts you're currently carrying at whatever rates they sit at. It's worth running this exact calculation, right now, on every balance you owe, before reading any further — because the payoff-order strategy in the next two chapters only works if you know, debt by debt, what each one is really costing you.

A second worked example, at a smaller balance

The mechanism doesn't only show up on large balances — it's just as real, proportionally, on a debt small enough to feel almost not worth worrying about. Take a $1,400 balance on a store card at 27% APR, a common rate for retail-branded cards, with a minimum payment starting around $42. At that minimum, shrinking as the balance shrinks, the payoff stretches past eight years, with total interest paid landing somewhere close to $1,100 — nearly as much as the original purchase itself, on a balance that felt too small to plan around.

Raise the fixed payment to $75 a month and the picture changes completely: payoff time drops to about 22 months, and total interest paid falls to roughly $220. An $1,100 lifetime interest bill becomes a $220 one, for a payment increase of about $33 a month, held steady instead of allowed to shrink. This is the pattern worth internalizing before moving to the next chapter: the size of the balance is almost never the thing that determines whether a debt is expensive. The gap between the minimum payment and a fixed, held payment is.

Why compounding frequency matters more than most people realize

Two credit cards can advertise the identical 22% APR and cost meaningfully different amounts over the same balance and payment schedule, purely because of how often interest compounds. Most major credit card issuers compound interest daily, meaning the stated APR gets divided into a daily periodic rate, applied to the balance every single day, with each day's interest added to the balance that the next day's interest gets calculated against. A card compounding monthly instead of daily, at the identical stated APR, produces a slightly lower effective annual cost, because there are fewer compounding events per year for interest to build on interest.

The gap between daily and monthly compounding at the same headline rate is usually modest in percentage terms — often under half a percentage point of real annual difference — but it's a real, calculable difference, and it's one more reason the APR printed at the top of a statement is a starting point for understanding a debt's true cost, not the complete answer. The practical takeaway isn't that compounding frequency should drive which card to pay off first (the difference is rarely large enough to reorder a payoff sequence on its own) — it's that

"22% APR" on two different cards is not always a perfectly apples-to-apples comparison, and knowing that keeps you appropriately skeptical of any calculation that treats the headline rate as the whole story.

The difference between APR and interest rate, and why the distinction matters most on installment loans

On revolving credit like credit cards, APR and interest rate are effectively the same figure for practical purposes. On installment loans — personal loans, auto loans, some student loans — the two can diverge, because APR is designed to capture the total annualized cost of borrowing, including certain fees rolled into the loan, while the interest rate alone reflects only the rate applied to the outstanding principal. An auto loan advertised at a 6% interest rate might carry an APR of 6.4% or higher once an origination fee or a documentation fee is factored in — a small gap in this example, but a real one, and exactly the kind of gap that matters when comparing two different loan offers rather than evaluating a single loan in isolation.

This is precisely why the four-question consolidation test from Chapter 5 insists on total-interest-cost comparison rather than a simple rate comparison — APR already captures more of the real cost than a bare interest rate does, but even APR doesn't capture everything (it typically doesn't reflect a truly comprehensive picture of every possible fee, particularly ones triggered only under certain conditions, like a late fee or an early-payoff penalty on loans that carry one). The only fully reliable comparison between two lending offers is the total-dollars-paid comparison this book returns to repeatedly — not the interest rate, and not even the APR, taken alone.

Fees hiding inside "interest-free" arrangements

A distinct trap sits alongside the minimum-payment mechanics already covered: some debt arrangements marketed as interest-free still carry real costs disguised as something other than interest — a monthly account maintenance fee on certain retail financing plans, a mandatory add-on insurance or warranty product bundled into a payment plan's total cost, or a processing fee charged on every payment made through a specific channel. None of these show up in an APR disclosure, because none of them are technically interest, but all of them function identically to interest from the borrower's perspective: a real, recurring cost of carrying the balance, paid regardless of the headline "0%" or "interest-free" label attached to the arrangement.

The corrective is the same one this chapter has returned to throughout: calculate the true total cost, not just the labeled interest rate. Add up every recurring fee across the full term of any "interest-free" arrangement and compare that total against what a standard, appropriately-labeled loan or credit line would have cost for the identical amount over the identical period. In a meaningful number of cases, a genuinely interest-free arrangement with an attached monthly fee ends up costing more, in real total dollars, than a modest-interest personal loan would have — a comparison that's invisible unless the fees are deliberately pulled out and totaled separately from the marketed 0% rate.

The illusion of progress: why a shrinking minimum payment feels like good news

There's a specific, worth-naming psychological wrinkle built into the minimum-payment structure described earlier in this chapter, and it's tactical rather than diagnostic, which is why it belongs here rather than being waved off as outside this book's scope. As a revolving balance slowly declines under minimum-only payments, the minimum payment itself — calculated as a percentage of the current balance — declines right along with it. A statement showing a smaller required payment than the one before it reads, at a glance, like a sign of progress: the bill is shrinking, therefore things are improving. The balance underneath, however, is often barely moving, precisely because a shrinking payment is also doing proportionally less work against the principal each month.

This isn't a coincidence of the formula — it's the direct, mechanical explanation for why a minimum-payment strategy can feel, month over month, like quiet improvement while actually representing a debt on pace to take over a decade to clear. The corrective is simple and already built into this chapter's framework: track total balance remaining, not the size of the required minimum payment, as the actual measure of progress. A minimum payment shrinking while a balance stays flat is not evidence of anything positive — it's the visible symptom of the exact mechanism this chapter opened by describing.

Prepayment penalties: the exception that can flip the math

A detail worth flagging explicitly, since it can materially affect the extra-payment strategy this entire book is built around: some installment loans, particularly certain personal loans, older auto loans, and in some cases mortgages, include a **prepayment penalty** — a fee charged specifically for paying off a loan earlier than its scheduled term, designed to compensate the lender for the interest income it loses when a loan is paid down faster than expected. This isn't universal — many modern consumer loans in the U.S. carry no prepayment penalty at all, and it's often a selling point lenders advertise explicitly — but it isn't rare enough to assume away either, and it directly affects the extra-payment math throughout this book.

Before applying any accelerated extra payment to an installment loan under the Chapter 3 payoff order, check the loan's specific terms for a prepayment penalty clause. If one exists, run the comparison explicitly: does the interest saved by paying the loan off early still exceed the penalty charged for doing so? In the large majority of real cases, particularly on shorter-term consumer loans, the interest saved comfortably exceeds any prepayment penalty, and the accelerated payment remains the right move — but it's a five-minute check worth making before assuming it, rather than after making a large extra payment and being surprised by a fee taken out of what should have been pure savings.

Penalty APR: the cost of a single late payment, made concrete

Most credit card agreements include a provision for a **penalty APR** — a substantially higher interest rate, sometimes well above the card's standard purchase rate, triggered by a payment that arrives late past a certain threshold (commonly 60 days past due, though terms vary by issuer and cardholder agreement). Once triggered, a penalty APR can apply not only going forward but, in some cases, to the existing balance as well, and it can remain in effect for an extended period — commonly at least six months of on-time payments before the account may qualify for a reduction back toward the standard rate, at the issuer's discretion.

This is worth understanding as the sharpest, most concrete illustration of why this book's repeated emphasis on paying every minimum payment on every account, regardless of its rank in the payoff order, isn't a minor administrative footnote — it's a direct defense against a single missed payment converting an already-expensive debt into a dramatically more expensive one, for a period measured in months, at the exact moment a payoff plan is trying to accelerate progress rather than lose ground to a self-inflicted rate increase. If a penalty APR does get triggered despite best efforts, it's worth revisiting the Chapter 4 negotiation scripts directly — asking explicitly to have the penalty rate reduced or removed after a documented run of on-time payments is a normal, reasonable request, and issuers grant it often enough that it's always worth asking rather than assuming the elevated rate is permanent.

Reading your own amortization schedule

Most loan servicers — for installment debt specifically, such as auto loans, personal loans, and student loans — provide an amortization schedule on request, or make one viewable directly in the account portal, showing the exact principal-versus-interest split for every remaining payment through the end of the loan term. This is worth pulling for any installment loan you're carrying, because it makes the abstract concept from this chapter's mechanics section concrete and specific to your actual account: you can see, for your exact loan, precisely how many of your dollars this month are going toward the balance versus the bank, and precisely how that ratio shifts as the loan matures.

A useful, specific thing to look for on your own amortization schedule: the exact month at which the principal-to-interest split crosses fifty percent — the point after which more than half of each regular payment starts reducing the balance rather than covering interest. On a long-term loan, particularly a mortgage (which this book doesn't cover in depth, since it's typically a different category of financial decision than the shorter-horizon consumer debt this book focuses on, but the mechanism is identical), that crossover point can sit years into the loan's life. Knowing where your specific crossover point falls tells you precisely how much leverage an extra payment made today actually carries — an extra payment made before that crossover point is disproportionately valuable, because it's eliminating principal at the exact stage of the loan where the regular payment itself is doing the least of that work.

Grace periods and cash advances: two exceptions to the standard rate

Two structural details are worth understanding precisely, because they change the real cost calculation in ways a simple balance-and-rate view misses.

Grace periods apply to new purchases on most credit cards, meaning interest doesn't accrue on a new charge if the full statement balance is paid by the due date. This grace period disappears entirely the moment any balance carries over month to month — once interest is accruing on a balance, new purchases typically start accruing interest immediately, from the date of purchase, with no grace period at all, until the full balance (old and new) is paid off completely. This is a meaningful, often-missed detail: a card that felt interest-free for years of full-balance payments can start charging interest on every single new purchase the moment even one balance carries over, and that shift is invisible unless you know to look for it in the account terms.

Cash advances — using a credit card to withdraw cash, or certain transactions treated as cash-equivalent, such as some money transfers or gambling transactions — typically carry a separate, higher APR than the card's purchase rate, begin accruing interest immediately with no grace period regardless of the account's overall payment status, and often include an additional flat or percentage-based fee charged at the time of the transaction. A cash advance is, mechanically, one of the most expensive ways to borrow money available through a normal consumer credit card, and it's worth checking your card's specific terms before ever using this feature, even in a genuine emergency — a personal loan or even a collections negotiation, covered in Chapter 4, is very often a cheaper path to the same cash.

The order in which you attack multiple debts is the next lever, and it's a bigger one than most people ever pull.

Chapter 2 — Avalanche vs. Snowball: The Real Math

The situation

Picture someone carrying four separate balances: a $9,000 credit card at 24% APR, a $4,500 car loan at 7% APR, a $2,000 medical bill at 0% APR on a payment plan, and a $1,200 store card at 26% APR. They have $600 a month to put toward debt beyond the minimums, and they've read two conflicting pieces of advice — pay the highest interest rate first, or pay the smallest balance first — from two sources that each present their method as the only correct one. Both can't be right, and the honest answer is that both are right about different things, which is exactly the kind of answer that gets lost when advice gets simplified into a slogan.

The mechanics

Both methods share the same foundation, and it's worth stating clearly because it's the part that never changes regardless of which order you choose: pay the minimum on every single debt except one. Direct every extra dollar you have — the $600 in the example above — at exactly one debt at a time, in full, until it's gone. Then roll that entire freed-up payment (its old minimum plus whatever extra you were paying) onto the next debt in your chosen order. This is often called "rolling the snowball" regardless of which method you're using, because the payment amount grows as each debt clears, the same way a snowball rolling downhill picks up size. The only thing that differs between avalanche and snowball is which debt you target first, second, third.

The debt avalanche targets the highest interest rate first, regardless of balance size. In the example above, that means the 26% store card gets the extra $600 first (despite being the smallest balance), then the 24% credit card, then the 7% car loan, with the 0% medical bill paid at its minimum the entire time since it costs nothing extra to carry. This order is mathematically guaranteed to minimize total interest paid and total time to debt-free, for a fixed total monthly payment, every single time, without exception. It is not a matter of opinion or which expert you trust — it's a direct consequence of how compound interest works. Attacking the highest rate first means every dollar you send that direction stops the fastest-growing balance from growing, which by definition saves the most money of any possible sequencing.

The debt snowball, popularized as a behavioral strategy rather than a mathematically optimal one, targets the smallest balance first regardless of interest rate. In the example above, that means the $1,200 store card gets the extra $600 first (which happens to also be the highest-rate debt here, but that's coincidental — in a different set of numbers the smallest balance and highest rate wouldn't overlap), then the $2,000 medical bill, then the $4,500 car loan, then the $9,000 credit card last. The stated rationale isn't mathematical optimization — it's that clearing an entire account, start to finish, produces a concrete win faster than the avalanche method usually does, and that win is treated as fuel for continuing rather than as a minor consolation prize.

Here's the part worth being precise about, because it's where most explanations get sloppy: the snowball method is not free. It costs real money in additional interest compared to the avalanche, in every case where the smallest balance and the highest rate aren't the same debt. The size of that cost is a knowable, calculable number — not a vague "a little more," but an actual dollar figure you can compute for your own situation before choosing. Whether that cost is worth paying is a real question this book will answer directly in Chapter 7, but it should never be answered by pretending the cost doesn't exist.

The framework

Here's how to actually run both calculations on your own debts, so you're choosing with real numbers instead of picking a side based on which book you read first.

Step one: list every debt with three numbers — current balance, APR, and minimum payment. Put them in a simple table, on paper or in a spreadsheet.

Step two: sort the list two ways. Make one copy sorted by APR, highest to lowest (your avalanche order). Make a second copy sorted by balance, smallest to largest (your snowball order).

Step three: simulate both, month by month, using your real extra-payment amount. For each order, apply minimums to every debt, then the full extra amount to whichever debt is first in that order. When a debt clears, roll its payment into the next one. Continue until everything's paid off. Track two numbers for each simulation: total months to debt-free, and total interest paid across all debts combined. A basic spreadsheet with a few formulas handles this cleanly, and several free online debt-payoff calculators will run this simulation automatically once you enter your balances, rates, and extra payment amount — you don't need to build the spreadsheet by hand if you don't want to, but understanding what it's doing under the hood is what lets you trust the output.

Step four: compare the two totals side by side. This is the number that actually informs the decision — not which method sounds more disciplined, but the real dollar gap and real time gap between the two, for your specific balances.

The worked example

Back to the four debts: $9,000 at 24%, $4,500 at 7%, $2,000 at 0%, $1,200 at 26%, with $600 a month total extra beyond minimums.

Running the avalanche order (26% card, then 24% card, then 7% car loan, with the 0% medical bill on its own minimum track throughout) against the snowball order (which in this case starts with the same 26% card since it's both smallest and highest-rate, then the 0% medical bill, then the 7% car loan, then the 24% card last) produces a real, calculable gap. In cases like this one, where the smallest-balance debt and highest-rate debt happen to be the same account, the two methods start identically and only diverge on the second target — the snowball clears the 0% medical debt next (which was already free to carry, so accelerating it saves zero interest) while the avalanche moves to the 24% card next (which is actively costing money every month it's not paid down). That divergence point is where the avalanche starts pulling ahead in total interest saved, typically landing somewhere in the range of a few hundred to a bit over a thousand dollars less in total interest paid across the full payoff period, depending on exact balances and how long the higher-rate debt is allowed to keep accruing under the snowball's order. The total payoff timeline for both methods lands close together in a case like this, within a month or two of each other, because the total debt and total payment are identical

— the real difference here shows up almost entirely in total interest, not overall speed.

The gap tells a different story when the numbers don't line up as neatly. If the largest balance also carries the highest rate — say a $12,000 card at 27% sitting alongside a $1,500 card at 19% — the avalanche and snowball orders diverge immediately and the interest gap grows substantially larger, because the snowball spends its early months clearing a cheap, small debt while the expensive, large one keeps compounding untouched. In that shape of situation, the avalanche's advantage over the snowball can run into several thousand dollars over the life of the full payoff, not a few hundred — which is exactly why running your own numbers, rather than trusting either method as a universal rule, matters more than picking a side on principle.

The honest takeaway: avalanche wins on pure math, always, without exception, and the size of that win depends entirely on how your specific balances and rates are arranged relative to each other — sometimes a rounding error, sometimes thousands of dollars. Snowball wins on something math can't measure directly — whether you actually stick with the plan for the two, three, five years it might take — and Chapter 7 will give that question the real, tactical treatment it deserves rather than treating it as an afterthought.

Handling irregular income and variable extra payments

Both simulations in this chapter's framework assume, for simplicity, a fixed extra-payment amount every month. Real income is often less consistent than that — commission-based work, freelance or gig income, seasonal employment, or any household with month-to-month variability in what's genuinely available beyond fixed expenses. It's worth addressing directly how the avalanche and snowball math holds up under irregular income, because the underlying logic doesn't actually require a fixed monthly figure to function correctly.

The core rule survives irregular income entirely intact: whatever extra amount is available in a given month, regardless of size, goes to the current target debt in your chosen order, in full, before any of it gets split or redirected elsewhere. A strong month with significant surplus accelerates the current target debt further; a lean month with little or no surplus just means less progress that month, without requiring any change to the order itself. The mistake worth avoiding specifically under irregular income is treating a lean month as a reason to abandon or pause the plan altogether, rather than contributing whatever's honestly available that month and returning to a larger contribution when the next strong month arrives — the order and the mechanism keep working at any payment size, including very small ones in a genuinely tight month, as long as the process itself continues rather than stopping.

For genuinely volatile income, it's also worth building a slightly larger buffer into the emergency-fund thinking from Chapter 9 earlier than that chapter's framework would otherwise suggest — someone with unpredictable income benefits from having buffer available during the active payoff period itself, not only after debt-free status is reached, precisely because a lean-income month combined with an unplanned expense is a more common, more foreseeable combination for irregular earners than for salaried ones.

A third method, mentioned here without being recommended as a default

Beyond avalanche, snowball, and the hybrid covered in the next chapter, a third approach shows up occasionally in personal finance discussions: **debt stacking by monthly payment size** rather than by balance or rate — attacking whichever debt has the highest minimum payment first, on the logic that eliminating it frees up the most monthly cash flow fastest, improving month-to-month breathing room even before any debt is fully paid off.

This method solves a real problem — cash-flow pressure, distinct from total-interest-cost or motivation — that neither avalanche nor snowball directly targets. Someone whose primary constraint is monthly cash flow, rather than total interest paid or psychological momentum, might reasonably weigh this factor into their own version of the hybrid framework in Chapter 3, treating "frees up the most monthly minimum fastest" as an additional, situational adjustment layered on top of the rate-and-small-balance logic already covered. It's not presented as a fourth full method with its own chapter, because for most people the mathematically optimal avalanche order and the psychologically sustainable hybrid order already address the two variables that matter most — but if monthly cash-flow pressure specifically is your binding constraint rather than either interest cost or motivation, this variable exists and can be incorporated directly into your own version of the framework.

Why the gap between the two methods varies so much from person to person

It's worth being explicit about what actually determines whether the avalanche-versus-snowball gap is trivial or enormous for a given set of debts, because the size of that gap is not random — it's a direct function of three measurable properties of your specific debt list.

The rate spread — the difference between your highest and lowest interest rates — is the single biggest driver. A debt list where every balance sits between 18% and 24% will show a small avalanche-versus-snowball gap, because there's not much difference in cost regardless of which one you attack first. A debt list that spans, say, a 3% auto loan and a 29% store card shows a large gap, because the order in which those two specific debts get attacked matters enormously.

The correlation between balance size and rate matters just as much, and it's the part most explanations skip. When your smallest balance also happens to carry your highest rate — a common pattern, since store cards and smaller retail-financing balances often carry the highest rates in a typical portfolio — the avalanche and snowball orders start out identical, and the gap between them stays small, sometimes negligible. When your smallest balance carries a low rate and your largest balance carries a high rate — a less common but real pattern, sometimes seen when someone has a large, high-rate credit card balance alongside a smaller, low-rate personal loan — the two methods diverge sharply from the very first month, and the gap grows large.

The total extra-payment amount available each month also matters, though less obviously. A larger extra payment shortens the entire payoff timeline for both methods, which means less total time for the "wrong" debt to keep accruing interest under either order — shrinking the absolute dollar gap between the two approaches even when the rate spread is wide. A smaller extra payment stretches the timeline for both, giving the mis-ordered debt more months to compound, which widens the gap.

None of this changes the core rule from earlier in this chapter — avalanche is always at least as good as snowball, mathematically, and usually strictly better — but it does mean the size of the tradeoff you're making by choosing snowball or hybrid over pure avalanche is worth actually calculating for your own numbers rather than assuming it's always large or always trivial. Both assumptions are wrong often enough to matter.

Why avalanche's advantage shrinks as the extra payment shrinks toward the total minimums

One counterintuitive pattern worth understanding directly: the avalanche method's dollar advantage over the snowball tends to shrink, in percentage terms, as the total extra payment available grows very large relative to the total debt — a large enough extra payment clears everything quickly enough, under either order, that there's simply not much time for any debt to compound meaningfully regardless of sequence. The inverse is also true and matters more in practice: a very small extra payment, just barely above the combined minimums, stretches the payoff timeline for both methods substantially, giving the highest-rate debt far more time to compound under a mis-ordered snowball sequence — which means the avalanche's advantage is often largest, in real dollar terms, for exactly the situations where money is tightest and an extra dollar of interest saved matters most.

This is worth internalizing as a general rule rather than just a one-off observation: the value of getting the order right is not a luxury consideration relevant mainly to larger, more comfortable extra payments. It's most valuable, in absolute dollar terms, precisely when the extra payment available is smallest and the total payoff timeline is longest — which is also, often, exactly the situation of someone who can least afford to leave real money on the table through a suboptimal order.

A second worked example, with a wider rate spread

Take a different four-debt profile: a $2,000 personal loan at 9% APR, an $8,500 credit card at 26% APR, a $1,000 medical bill at 0%, and a $15,000 auto loan at 5% APR, with $700 a month available beyond minimums.

Here, the smallest balance ($1,000 medical bill) is 0% — already excluded from either race, since accelerating it saves no interest. The next-smallest balance ($2,000 personal loan) sits at a moderate 9%, while the largest interest-bearing balance ($8,500 credit card) carries by far the highest rate at 26%.

Under snowball order, the $2,000 personal loan gets attacked first despite its relatively low rate, delaying the start of paying down the $8,500 card at 26% by several months. Under avalanche order, the $8,500 card gets attacked immediately, and the 9% personal loan waits. Running both simulations, the gap here lands substantially larger than in the earlier example — often several thousand dollars in additional interest under snowball, precisely because the rate spread is wide (26% versus 9%) and the correlation between balance size and rate runs in the "expensive" direction, with a meaningful balance sitting at the highest rate rather than the lowest. This is exactly the profile where running the actual numbers before choosing a method matters most, because the felt difference between the two orders — "pay the smaller one first" versus "pay the higher-rate one first" — sounds similar in plain language but produces a materially different financial outcome underneath.

For now, the job is simpler: run both simulations on your real numbers, and know the actual size of the gap between them before you decide anything. Chapter 3 builds the exact payoff order from there, including a hybrid approach that captures most of the avalanche's savings without asking you to ignore the psychological reality the snowball is built around.

Chapter 3 — Building Your Exact Payoff Order

The situation

Someone finishes Chapter 2, runs both simulations on their own five debts, and finds the avalanche saves $2,100 in interest over the snowball but the smallest debt under the avalanche order won't clear for eleven months, because it happens to carry the lowest rate of the five. They liked the idea of a fast first win. Now they're stuck choosing between a plan that saves real money and a plan that might actually hold their attention — and they've been told, by two different camps, that this is an either-or decision. It isn't. There's a third order that exists specifically for this situation, and almost no mainstream debt advice mentions it by name.

The mechanics

The **hybrid payoff order** — sometimes called a modified avalanche or a blended method, though it has no single standardized name — works by applying one adjustment rule on top of a pure avalanche sort: any debt below a certain small-balance threshold (a reasonable default is anything that would clear within one to three months at your extra-payment amount) gets moved to the front of the line, ahead of its interest-rate rank, and every debt above that threshold stays sorted by rate exactly as the avalanche method prescribes.

The logic is straightforward once it's stated plainly: a debt that's going to clear in six weeks regardless of where you rank it costs you almost nothing in extra interest by going first, because it's barely going to be alive long enough to accrue meaningful interest either way. But it buys you the exact thing the pure avalanche order doesn't guarantee — an early, real, complete payoff, with a zeroed-out account and a canceled card, inside the first couple of months instead of however many months the avalanche's rate-only sort happens to produce.

This isn't a compromise that costs you the avalanche's mathematical advantage in any meaningful way, and that's the part worth understanding precisely rather than taking on faith. The interest cost of moving a near-zero balance to the front is small by construction — you defined the threshold specifically so that the amount of extra interest the higher-rate debts accrue during those few extra weeks is trivial relative to the full payoff, typically single or low double digits in dollars, not hundreds. You're not choosing between "all the savings" and "an early win." In most real debt profiles, you're choosing between "all the savings" and "97-99% of the savings, plus an early win" — which is a much easier trade to make honestly.

There's a second adjustment to make here, distinct from the small-balance threshold: **the zero-interest exception**. Any debt sitting at a true 0% promotional or payment-plan rate (a common structure for medical bills and some retail financing) should always be paid at its minimum only, regardless of balance size, and never accelerated ahead of any interest-bearing debt — accelerating a 0% balance produces zero interest savings by definition, so any extra dollar sent there instead of to an interest-bearing debt is a dollar that earned you nothing it couldn't have earned elsewhere. The only exception to the zero-interest exception is a hard deadline: if a 0% promotional period has a known expiration after which the rate jumps sharply, treat the remaining balance as high-priority in the final month or two before that expiration, timed so the debt clears before the rate resets — not because it's urgent now, but because it's about to stop being a 0% debt at all.

The framework

Here's the four-step process for building your own exact order.

Step one: list every debt with balance, APR, and minimum payment, exactly as in Chapter 2.

Step two: flag any true 0% debts and set them aside to minimum-only payments, noting any promotional expiration date if one exists.

Step three: sort the remaining debts by APR, highest to lowest — this is your avalanche baseline.

Step four: identify any debt that would clear within roughly one to three months at your extra-payment amount, and move it to the very front of the order, ahead of every other interest-bearing debt regardless of rate. If more than one debt qualifies under that threshold, order those early debts by balance, smallest first, so you bank the fastest possible sequence of quick wins before shifting into pure rate-order for the rest of the list.

The result is your locked payoff order — the specific sequence you'll follow start to finish, revisited only if a rate changes materially (a variable-rate card's APR moves, for instance) or a new debt gets added to the list.

The worked example

Take five debts: a $600 medical copay plan at 0% (no expiration, ongoing), a $900 store card at 27% APR, a $7,200 credit card at 21% APR, a $3,000 personal loan at 13% APR, and a $11,500 car loan at 6.5% APR. Extra payment available: $500 a month beyond all minimums.

Pure avalanche order would run: store card (27%) → credit card (21%) → personal loan (13%) → car loan (6.5%), with the medical plan on minimum-only throughout since it's 0%. That's mathematically optimal, full stop.

Now apply the hybrid rule. At $500 extra a month plus its own minimum, the $900 store card clears in under two months — it already qualifies as the first target under pure avalanche anyway, since it's also the highest rate, so nothing changes there. But suppose the numbers were arranged differently: a $650 store card at 15% and a $7,200 credit card at 24%. Pure avalanche would hit the 24% card first, and the small 15% store card would sit, unpaid beyond its minimum, until every higher-rate debt cleared — potentially over a year later. The hybrid rule pulls that $650 balance to the front instead, clearing it in about two months, at a real, calculable cost of roughly $10-15 in extra interest on the 24% card during that short delay. Two months in, there's a fully closed account, a small confidence win, and a freed-up minimum payment rolling into the next target — for a cost of about the price of a movie ticket in extra interest paid. That's the actual trade, in real numbers, not a vague gesture at "a little less optimal."

Sharing the plan across a household without losing precision

Where a payoff plan involves more than one household member's buy-in — a shared decision even when the debt itself might sit on one person's individual accounts — it's worth translating the exact order from this chapter's framework into a format that's genuinely legible to someone who hasn't read the preceding chapters closely. A simple, shared one-page document works well: every debt listed in its locked order, the current balance and rate next to each, the extra-payment amount currently being applied, and a running combined-total number (the same tracking metric recommended in Chapter 7) updated on the same fixed monthly cadence recommended elsewhere in this book.

This kind of shared document does two specific things. First, it prevents the specific coordination failure covered later in this book (Chapter 8's household-coordination note) — two people independently making decisions about "their" debt without a shared, current picture of the whole. Second, it turns household accountability, discussed as a tactical tool in Chapter 7, into something concrete and specific rather than a vague shared intention — a real, current document that both people can look at together on a fixed date, rather than a general sense that "we're working on the debt" with no shared, precise reference point for what that actually means this month.

Handling a debt that doesn't fit neatly into the sort

Occasionally a debt shows up on a list that resists a clean rate comparison against the others — a promissory note to a family member with no formal interest rate attached, a buy-now-pay-later plan with a short, fixed 0% window and a hard deadline, or an old collections account with a listed balance that's ambiguous because of accumulated fees. Each of these deserves a specific, deliberate placement decision rather than being forced into the standard rate sort by guesswork.

A no-interest family loan, if truly interest-free and with no rigid repayment schedule imposed by the lender, functions similarly to the 0% medical debt already covered — minimum-only or even lowest priority in the objective math, though it's worth being honest that family lending carries a real relational cost to leaving unpaid indefinitely that a pure numbers framework doesn't capture, and that's a legitimate, non-mechanical factor worth weighing on its own terms rather than pretending it doesn't exist. A buy-now-pay-later plan with a hard deadline should be treated the way this book treats any 0% debt with an expiration date, covered in Chapter 3's zero-interest exception — minimum-only until close to the deadline, then prioritized specifically to clear before the window closes and any deferred interest or fee structure kicks in, since many buy-now-pay-later products carry retroactive interest charges if the full balance isn't cleared by the deadline, a detail worth confirming directly in the plan's terms. An old collections balance with an unclear fee structure is best handled by first sending the written validation request described in Chapter 4, establishing the actual, current, accurate balance before it gets assigned any rank in the payoff order at all — sorting an inflated or disputed balance into your plan before resolving the dispute risks paying more than necessary or misallocating extra payments toward a number that shouldn't be that large in the first place.

Building the payoff order into a real budget, not just a list

The hybrid order from this chapter answers "which debt gets the extra payment first." It doesn't, by itself, answer where the extra payment amount comes from in the first place — a separate question this book has deliberately treated as a given input throughout, since general budgeting mechanics are covered well elsewhere and aren't this book's specific job. Briefly, though, here's how the extra-payment figure should be set, since an unrealistic figure undermines everything built on top of it.

A workable, conservative approach: calculate the extra-payment amount from actual, verified surplus — income minus every fixed and typical variable expense, reviewed across at least one or two real recent months rather than an aspirational budget that assumes spending will change starting immediately. An extra-payment figure set from an aspirational budget that hasn't actually been tested tends to be too optimistic, and an extra-payment amount that isn't sustainable in practice undermines the entire structure this chapter has built, regardless of how well-designed the payoff order itself is. It's better to set a conservative, verified extra-payment amount and occasionally add a bonus payment when genuine surplus appears, than to commit to an aggressive number on paper that quietly starts getting skipped a few months in.

A related practical point: build a small buffer into the extra-payment figure rather than committing every last available dollar to the plan. A payoff plan with zero slack turns any minor, ordinary month-to-month expense variation into a missed extra payment and a small, avoidable disruption to the plan's momentum. A payoff plan with even a modest built-in buffer absorbs that same ordinary variation without any disruption at all — the extra payment simply happens as planned, drawing on the buffer rather than requiring the month to have gone perfectly.

What to do when a rate changes mid-plan

Payoff orders aren't always static for the full life of the plan, and it's worth having a rule ready for the most common disruption: a variable-rate card's APR moves, usually upward, tied to broader rate cycles. When this happens, the correct response is mechanical, not emotional — re-run step three of the framework (the rate sort) with the updated number, check whether the debt's new rank in the order has changed relative to your other debts, and adjust the sequence only if it has. A rate move of a percentage point or two rarely changes a debt's rank meaningfully. A larger jump — several points at once, which does happen, particularly on cards with rates tied to an underlying benchmark rate that itself moved sharply — can genuinely change where a debt belongs in the order, and it's worth the two minutes it takes to re-check rather than assuming the original order still holds.

The same logic applies, in reverse, to any debt that gets partially paid down unexpectedly — a bonus, a tax refund, a gift applied directly to one balance. Re-run the small-balance threshold check from step four after any large one-time payment, since a debt that didn't originally qualify for the front-of-line quick-win treatment might now be close enough to warrant moving up.

A note on debts you're tempted to skip entirely

There's a specific trap some people fall into once a payoff order is built: treating the debts ranked last as effectively invisible until every debt ahead of them clears. This is correct in terms of where extra payment dollars go, but it's incorrect in terms of attention — every debt in the order still needs its minimum paid, on time, every single month, regardless of its rank. A missed minimum payment on a low-priority debt, made simply because it felt unimportant relative to the debt getting the extra attention, can trigger a penalty APR increase, a late fee, and real damage to credit standing — costs that can easily exceed whatever the small delay in reaching that debt in the payoff order was supposed to save. The payoff order determines where extra money goes. It does not change the requirement that every account, in every position, gets its minimum paid without fail.

This is the order this book recommends building for yourself, debt by debt, before moving to the next three chapters — because negotiation, consolidation, and balance transfers all work by changing the numbers that go into this exact framework, not by replacing it. Get the order locked first. Everything from here forward is about making the individual debts in that order cheaper, faster, or both.

Chapter 4 — Negotiating With Creditors and Collections

The situation

A credit card statement doesn't include a phone number for "call to ask for a lower rate," and most people never call one that exists on the back of the card either, because it doesn't occur to them that the number on the statement is negotiable at all. It looks like a fixed term, printed and final, the same way a price tag looks fixed in a store that doesn't haggle. Interest rates on unsecured debt are, in a meaningful number of cases, more negotiable than most people assume — not infinitely, not always, but enough that never asking is a real, quantifiable mistake made by a large share of people carrying revolving debt.

A different, more urgent version of this situation: an account has gone to collections, and the calls have started. The person answering has two instincts, both understandable and both often costly — either avoid the calls entirely, which lets the debt sit, potentially escalate to a lawsuit, and continue affecting credit standing, or answer and agree to whatever payment plan is proposed first, without knowing that collectors routinely have far more room to negotiate than their first offer reveals.

The mechanics

There's a legal and structural backdrop worth understanding before any script, because it changes how a conversation should be approached. In the United States, debt collection is governed by the Fair Debt Collection Practices Act (FDCPA), a federal law that restricts what collectors can say, when they can call, and how they must respond to certain requests — including a written request to verify a debt (a "debt validation" request), which a collector is required to honor before continuing collection activity, and a request to stop calling at a specific number or time. Knowing these rights doesn't just protect you from harassment — it establishes, from the first phone call, that you're someone who understands the process, which materially changes the tenor of the negotiation that follows.

Original creditors (the bank or issuer you originally borrowed from, before any account is sold to a third party) generally have the most flexibility on active, current accounts, because they'd rather keep you as a paying customer at a lower rate than lose the account to a competitor's balance transfer offer or a bankruptcy filing. This is the conversation to have on any account that's current or only mildly behind — before it's sold off, while the original lender still has an incentive to keep the relationship.

Debt buyers and collection agencies, by contrast, typically purchase delinquent debt for a fraction of its face value — often somewhere in the range of a few cents to a few dozen cents on the dollar, varying widely by debt age, type, and the individual portfolio purchased. This detail matters enormously for negotiation, because it means a debt buyer can accept a settlement well below the stated balance and still profit — their cost basis is nowhere near the number printed on the account. Understanding that gap is the single most useful piece of leverage in any collections negotiation: you are not negotiating against the original balance's true cost to the party you're speaking with. You're negotiating against what they actually paid for the account, which is almost always dramatically less.

Hardship programs exist at most major card issuers and lenders, typically temporary and requiring some documentation of a real hardship (job loss, medical event, reduced income), and they can include a reduced interest rate, a reduced minimum payment, or a temporary pause on payments without the account being reported delinquent. These programs are rarely advertised prominently and are almost always something you have to ask for by name.

The framework

Script one — rate reduction on a current account, spoken or in the issuer's chat/message system:

"I've been a customer for [X years/months] and I've noticed my rate is higher than some current offers I'm seeing elsewhere. I'd like to ask about a rate reduction on my account, or if there's a hardship or loyalty program I might qualify for. Is that something you're able to look into?"

Keep it short, factual, and free of apology. If the first representative says no, ask, politely, whether there's a retention or hardship department that handles this specifically — many front-line representatives don't have authority to adjust rates even when the account genuinely qualifies, and the retention team frequently does.

Script two — settlement negotiation with a collector, once a debt has gone to collections:

Before any settlement conversation, send a written debt validation request if you haven't already received clear written confirmation of the debt's amount, original creditor, and your right to dispute — this is a right under the FDCPA and it costs the collector time and paperwork to ignore, which alone sometimes produces better terms.

Once validated, the opening line: "I'm not able to pay the full balance, but I am able to resolve this. What's the best offer you can make for a lump-sum settlement?" Let them name a number first if possible — their first offer is rarely their floor. If they name a percentage of the balance, counter below it, and be prepared to walk the conversation to a second or third call rather than settling in the first exchange; collectors often have more room after a call is escalated internally than a first representative can offer on the spot.

One rule that overrides both scripts: get any negotiated agreement in writing before sending a single payment. A verbal agreement over the phone is not enforceable in any meaningful way if a dispute arises later, and settlement offers have, in real cases, been reneged on or misapplied when no written confirmation existed. Ask for the agreement in writing — email, a portal message, or physical mail — specifying the exact amount, the payment date, and explicit confirmation of how the account will be reported once paid, before you send money.

Lawsuits: what changes once a collector files

A meaningful share of collections accounts never escalate to a lawsuit, but some do, particularly on larger balances or accounts that have gone unaddressed for an extended period, and the mechanics of this chapter change directly once a summons has actually been filed and served, since the stakes and the correct response both shift materially at that point.

The single most important thing to know: a debt lawsuit that goes unanswered typically results in a default judgment against the defendant, which can lead to wage garnishment, a bank account levy, or a lien, depending on the jurisdiction's specific rules — and a default judgment happens specifically because no response was filed within the required window, not because the underlying debt was necessarily valid or the amount necessarily correct. Ignoring a lawsuit, in other words, converts what may have still been a negotiable situation into a legally enforced one, on the plaintiff's terms, essentially by forfeit. If a summons is received, the mechanically correct first step — regardless of whether a settlement was already in progress or being considered — is to file a timely response with the court by the stated deadline, even a brief one, to preserve the ability to negotiate, dispute, or defend at all. This is also the point at which consulting a consumer-law attorney, including free or low-cost legal aid resources available in many jurisdictions specifically for debt-collection defense, stops being optional caution and becomes a genuinely important step — the stakes and procedural requirements of an actual court filing go beyond what this book's negotiation scripts are built to handle safely on your own.

A written validation request, in full

Chapter 4's framework references sending a written debt validation request before a settlement negotiation, and it's worth providing the actual structure of one, since having the real shape of the request makes it far more likely to actually get sent rather than remaining a vague intention. A validation request, sent by mail (return receipt or a trackable delivery method is worth the small extra cost, since it creates a documented record of when the request was received) or through a collector's official written correspondence channel where available, should include: your name and the account or reference number provided by the collector, a clear statement requesting validation of the debt under the Fair Debt Collection Practices Act — specifically the original creditor's name, the original account number, an itemized accounting of the current balance including any fees or interest added since the account was opened or charged off, and confirmation of the collector's legal authority to collect the debt — and a request that all further communication occur in writing rather than by phone, if that's your preference.

Sending this request triggers a legal obligation for the collector to pause active collection activity until the requested validation is provided, and it accomplishes two things simultaneously: it protects you from continuing to be pursued on a debt that may be inaccurately recorded, inflated with improper fees, or in some cases entirely mistaken (debt records do get confused, duplicated, or misattributed more often than most people assume, particularly on older, resold accounts), and it establishes, from the first interaction, that you're operating from documentation rather than memory or assumption — which, as noted earlier in this chapter, tends to shift the tenor of every conversation that follows.

Building a settlement fund before you negotiate

Negotiating a settlement, as covered earlier in this chapter, is far more effective when a lump sum is actually available to offer, rather than negotiating a reduced balance you then still need to pay off gradually over time — a lump-sum settlement offer is a genuinely stronger negotiating position than a promise of a reduced-but-extended payment plan, because it gives the collector immediate, certain recovery rather than an extended stream of payments that carries its own risk of default.

For someone without a lump sum readily available, it's worth deliberately building one before initiating a settlement negotiation, rather than negotiating from a weaker position out of impatience. This can mean temporarily redirecting funds that would otherwise be going toward extra payments elsewhere in the Chapter 3 payoff order, specifically toward a dedicated settlement fund for a collections account — a legitimate, temporary deviation from the standard payoff order, justified by the fact that a successful settlement negotiation, funded by a real lump sum, often produces a larger total-dollar benefit than continuing standard extra payments elsewhere for the same few months. This is one of the few scenarios in this book where deliberately pausing the standard payoff order for a defined, short period is the mechanically correct move rather than a deviation to be corrected — but it should be a deliberate, calculated pause with a specific target and timeline, not an open-ended redirection.

How a settlement affects credit standing: a real tradeoff, stated plainly

A settled-for-less account is generally reported to credit bureaus differently than an account paid in full at the original balance — typically noted with a status like "settled" or "paid, settled" rather than "paid in full," a distinction visible to future lenders reviewing a credit report, and one that can have some effect on future credit decisions, though its practical impact varies and tends to fade in significance over time as the account ages. This is a real tradeoff, stated plainly rather than presenting the settlement scripts in this chapter as a costless win: a settlement typically saves real money today at some cost to how the account appears on a credit report for a period afterward, compared to paying the full balance over time.

Whether that tradeoff is worth making depends on your specific situation — someone planning a major credit application (a mortgage, in particular) in the near term may reasonably weigh this differently than someone with no major credit application planned, for whom the immediate dollar savings clearly outweighs a credit-report notation that will have diminishing relevance over the following months and years. Where possible, and it's always worth asking directly during the negotiation, request that the settled account be reported as "paid in full" rather than "settled" as part of the negotiated terms — some collectors will agree to this specific reporting language if asked directly, particularly when the settlement amount is close to the full balance, and it's a request that costs nothing to make.

The worked example

A $4,200 collections account, originally a credit card balance, now held by a debt buyer. The account holder sends a written validation request, receives confirmation of the debt within the required window, then calls to negotiate. The collector's opening offer: pay $3,600 over six months. The account holder, having read that debt buyers often pay a small fraction of face value, counters at a lump-sum offer of $1,470 (35% of the balance), payable within thirty days if she can gather the funds. The collector initially declines, offers $2,940 (70%), and after the account holder holds firm and asks to speak with a supervisor, the two sides land on $1,890 — 45% of the original balance, paid in one lump sum within two weeks, with written confirmation that the account will be reported as "settled in full" rather than left open or reported as still delinquent.

That's a $2,310 reduction from the original balance, achieved with two phone calls and one written request, on a debt that would otherwise have kept accruing collection fees and continued affecting her credit standing indefinitely. Not every negotiation lands at 45% — the real range varies widely by debt age, type, and the specific collector — but the mechanism behind that number, the gap between face value and what a debt buyer actually paid for the account, is real and worth using every time a collections call comes in, rather than accepting the first number offered.

A note on interest rate caps and usury limits

As background context for any negotiation, consumer interest rates in the United States are subject to a patchwork of state usury laws, though credit card issuers in particular are generally permitted to export the interest rate rules of the state where they're legally chartered, rather than the cardholder's home state — a structural detail explaining why credit card rates can run considerably higher than the usury caps that apply to some other loan types in the same state. This isn't directly actionable in the way a negotiation script is, but it's useful background for understanding why credit cards, specifically, tend to carry among the highest rates of any common consumer debt type discussed throughout this book, and why the rate-based avalanche logic in Chapter 2 so often ranks credit card debt at or near the top of a real payoff order — the rate structure isn't arbitrary or specific to any one issuer's pricing choices; it reflects a genuinely different regulatory treatment than most other consumer credit products receive.

What negotiating actually feels like, and why most people avoid it anyway

So few people who could benefit from these scripts ever use them, and it's not because of laziness or lack of information — both scripts above are freely available in some form across many financial resources. The reason is that the conversation itself feels adversarial, and most people are conflict-averse enough that a phone call framed as a confrontation gets avoided indefinitely, even when the avoidance is costing real money every month it continues.

The reframe worth adopting: this is not a confrontation, it's a business conversation between two parties with different information. The representative on the other end of a rate-reduction call is not personally invested in whether your rate stays high — they're following a script and a set of authorized actions, and asking a direct, calm, specific question is simply giving them the opening to use tools they already have. The collector on a settlement call is, in a very literal sense, doing their job by trying to recover the maximum amount possible, and you countering with a lower, calculated offer is not rude or unreasonable — it's the other half of a normal negotiation, one they have every single day with other account holders.

A practical tactic worth adding to both scripts: **never accept or reject an offer in the same call it's made, unless the number already meets your target.** Ask for time — "let me think about that and call back" is a complete, acceptable sentence in either type of call, and it accomplishes two things: it prevents an in-the-moment agreement to worse terms than you might get with a second call (representatives and collectors both sometimes have more authority to offer better terms on a follow-up or escalated call than on a first one), and it removes the social pressure of the live conversation from the actual decision, letting you evaluate the offer against your own numbers with a clear head.

When negotiation doesn't work, and what that actually means

Not every negotiation succeeds. Some original creditors have firm no-exception policies on rate adjustments tied to specific account tiers, and some debt buyers, particularly on very recently acquired accounts, may not yet have authorization to settle below a certain floor. A declined negotiation is worth treating as information, not failure — ask directly, if a representative declines, whether there's a specific waiting period after which the request could be reconsidered (some issuers have internal policies against multiple rate-reduction requests within a short window, meaning a request declined this month might succeed in three or six). Note the date, and calendar a follow-up.

It also matters to know when a settlement negotiation genuinely isn't the right tool, distinct from just not succeeding on a given call. A debt still held by the original creditor, current or only slightly late, is a different conversation than a charged-off account sold to a third-party buyer — the deep-discount settlement logic in this chapter's worked example applies specifically to the debt-buyer scenario, where the party you're negotiating with acquired the account for pennies on the dollar. Attempting the same aggressive settlement approach on a current account with the original creditor, who has full face-value exposure and often more interest in simply getting the account current again, tends to produce a hardship program or payment plan rather than a deep balance reduction — a genuinely useful outcome, just a mechanically different one. Know which conversation you're actually in before setting expectations on how much the balance itself might move.

Chapter 5 — The Truth About Debt Consolidation

The situation

Someone carrying four credit cards, total balance $18,000, average rate around 23%, gets a personal loan offer in the mail: consolidate everything into one loan at 11% APR, one monthly payment instead of four. On the surface, this looks like an obviously correct move — half the interest rate, simpler bookkeeping, one due date to track. In a meaningful share of real cases, it is a correct move. In another meaningful share, it quietly makes the situation worse, and the difference between the two outcomes comes down to a handful of mechanical details that the loan offer itself will never explain to you, because explaining them isn't in the lender's interest.

The mechanics

Debt consolidation, in its cleanest form, means replacing multiple debts with a single new loan at a lower blended interest rate, ideally with a fixed term and fixed payment. Done correctly, it can reduce total interest paid, simplify tracking, and — because installment loans typically report differently to credit bureaus than revolving credit card balances — sometimes improve a credit score by reducing what's called credit utilization (the percentage of your available revolving credit that's currently in use).

But three mechanical risks sit underneath that clean description, and each one, left unaddressed, can turn a consolidation loan from a genuine improvement into a net negative.

Risk one: the term-extension trap. A consolidation loan that lowers your monthly payment often does so by extending the repayment period, not just by lowering the rate. A shorter, higher-payment original debt load can end up costing less in total interest than a longer, lower-payment consolidated loan, even at a nominally better rate — because total interest is a function of rate multiplied by time, and stretching the time can offset or even exceed the benefit of a lower rate. This is not a hypothetical risk; it's the single most common way consolidation quietly fails to save money, and it's the one detail most consolidation offers are structured to obscure behind a smaller, more attractive-looking monthly payment number.

Risk two: the reopened-line relapse. Consolidating credit card debt into a personal loan pays off the cards, but doesn't close them (closing them can, in some cases, hurt a credit score by reducing available credit and shortening average account age — a genuinely separate and more nuanced decision). A newly-zeroed credit card is, mechanically, an open invitation to reaccumulate balance on top of a new consolidation loan, and this happens often enough that it deserves saying directly rather than assuming it won't apply to you: the original problem plus a new loan, rather than the original problem replaced by a better structure. This isn't a psychological failing unique to certain people — it's a structural risk built into the mechanism itself, and it's addressable with a concrete tactical step covered in the framework below, not just a warning to "be careful."

Risk three: fees that erase the rate advantage. Personal loans used for consolidation often carry an origination fee, commonly in the range of 1-8% of the loan amount, deducted up front or added to the balance. A loan advertised at an attractive rate can have its real, effective cost pushed meaningfully higher once the origination fee is factored in — and the only way to know the true comparison is to calculate the loan's effective APR including fees, not just read the advertised rate in isolation.

There's a fourth consideration specific to one debt type worth flagging clearly: **federal student loans consolidated into a private loan lose federal protections** — income-driven repayment options, deferment and forbearance provisions, and any current or future federal forgiveness programs — permanently and irreversibly. This is covered in more detail in Chapter 8, but it bears repeating here because it's the single highest-stakes version of the general consolidation-risk pattern: a lower headline rate can come attached to the permanent loss of protections that turn out to matter enormously if circumstances change later.

The framework

A four-question test to run on any consolidation offer before accepting it:

One: what's the new loan's total cost, not just its rate? Calculate total interest paid over the full new term, factoring in any origination fee, and compare that number directly against the total interest you'd pay following the payoff order from Chapters 2 and 3 without consolidating. If the consolidation's total cost is lower, it's a genuine improvement. If it's higher because of an extended term, it isn't — regardless of how much smaller the monthly payment looks.

Two: is the new term equal to or shorter than your realistic current payoff timeline? If the consolidation loan's term is longer than the time it would take to clear the current debts under your existing payoff order, treat that as a red flag requiring real justification (a genuine cash-flow need for a smaller payment, for instance) rather than accepting a longer timeline as a free byproduct of a lower rate.

Three: do you have a concrete plan for the reopened credit lines? Before consolidating any credit card debt, decide explicitly — will the cards be closed, frozen (physically or via an issuer's lock feature), left open but unused, or genuinely, disciplined-ly used for planned expenses only and paid in full monthly? Write the answer down. A consolidation plan without an explicit answer to this question is a plan built on hope rather than mechanics, and it's the single most common reason a first consolidation gets followed by a second one a few years later.

Four: are any of the debts being consolidated federal student loans? If yes, stop and read Chapter 8's dedicated treatment of student loan consolidation before proceeding — the calculus is materially different and the downside of an uninformed decision is larger and harder to reverse than with any other debt type.

The worked example

Back to the $18,000 across four cards, average 23% APR, current combined minimum payments totaling around $560 a month. A consolidation offer: $18,000 personal loan at 11% APR, 5-year term, 4% origination fee ($720, added to the loan balance for a total borrowed amount of $18,720), resulting monthly payment around $407.

Run the four-question test. Total interest over the 5-year term on the consolidated loan, including the fee-inflated balance, comes to roughly $5,600. Compare that against continuing the avalanche-ordered payoff on the original four cards at $560 a month (the same payment level as the current minimums combined, before any extra payment) — that route would take close to five years as well at that payment level, and total interest across the four cards, run through an avalanche simulation, lands in the range of $9,000-10,000 given the 23% average rate. On pure cost, the consolidation wins clearly — roughly $3,500-4,500 less in total interest, even after the origination fee.

But apply question three. Suppose the plan doesn't include an explicit answer for what happens to the four now-zeroed cards. Eighteen months later, without a concrete decision made up front, three of the four cards have new balances again, totaling $6,200 — spent gradually, on things that felt manageable one purchase at a time, on cards that were sitting open with available credit and no explicit plan attached to them. The consolidation loan itself is still performing exactly as designed, saving real money on the original $18,000. But the person is now carrying the consolidation payment plus $6,200 in new high-rate balances — a worse total position than if the original cards had simply been paid down under the Chapter 3 order with no consolidation at all. The loan mechanics weren't the failure. The absence of an explicit, written plan for the reopened lines was — which is exactly why question three isn't optional, and exactly why it's listed as a mechanical step, not a moral warning.

Co-signers and joint consolidation loans

Some consolidation loans, particularly for borrowers with a thinner or lower credit profile, become available or carry meaningfully better terms with a co-signer attached. It's worth understanding the mechanics of what a co-signer arrangement actually creates before asking someone to take on that role, or agreeing to take it on for someone else: a co-signer is not a reference or a character witness in any legal sense — they become fully, legally responsible for the debt exactly as if they had borrowed the money themselves, meaning a missed payment affects both the primary borrower's and the co-signer's credit history identically, and the co-signer remains liable for the full remaining balance regardless of any private, informal understanding about who's "really" responsible for making the payments.

This matters directly for the consolidation decision in this chapter: a co-signed consolidation loan should be evaluated using the identical four-question test as any other offer, but with an added, explicit conversation between both parties about what happens in exactly the failure scenarios this book has spent its chapters trying to prevent — a missed payment, a job loss, a dispute. Many lenders offer a co-signer release option after a defined period of consistent, on-time payments (commonly a year or more), and if a co-signed loan is the right move, confirm this release provision exists and understand its specific requirements before signing, rather than assuming the co-signer's obligation will simply and automatically end once the loan feels stable.

Shopping multiple lenders side by side, systematically

Because consolidation loan terms vary meaningfully across lenders for the identical borrower profile, as established earlier in this chapter, it's worth having a systematic way to compare offers rather than evaluating them one at a time as they arrive, which tends to anchor a decision too heavily on whichever offer happened to show up first. A simple comparison table — one row per lender, columns for APR, term, origination fee, total interest calculated under this chapter's four-question test, and monthly payment — built before accepting any single offer, turns a sequence of individually-evaluated mailers or emails into a genuine side-by-side comparison.

Most reputable lenders' prequalification tools, mentioned earlier in this chapter, allow gathering three or four real, personalized offers within a single sitting, using soft inquiries that don't affect your credit score. It's worth deliberately including at least one credit union and one online-only lender alongside any traditional bank offer in this comparison, since the earlier note about credit unions' typically favorable member rates and the generally faster, more automated underwriting some online lenders use for strong credit profiles both represent real, distinct pools of competitive offers worth checking rather than assuming a single, familiar bank's offer is representative of the market.

The credit-inquiry and account-age effects of consolidation, put in proportion

Applying for a consolidation loan generates a hard credit inquiry, and opening the resulting new loan affects average account age (a factor in most credit scoring models) — both real effects worth understanding, and both, in most cases, smaller and shorter-lived than people tend to assume. A single hard inquiry typically has a modest, temporary effect on a credit score, generally fading within several months and dropping off the report entirely after roughly two years. The reduction in average account age from adding one new loan is similarly modest for most credit profiles, particularly for someone with an established credit history predating the new consolidation loan by several years or more.

These effects deserve honest proportion, specifically because they're sometimes cited — inaccurately, in most real cases — as a reason to avoid consolidation altogether. The much larger, more consequential effect of a well-executed consolidation is usually the opposite: replacing several high-utilization revolving balances with one installment loan often *improves* a credit score, sometimes substantially, because revolving utilization (how much of your available revolving credit is currently in use) is typically weighted more heavily in common scoring models than the presence of one additional installment account. The short-term inquiry and account-age effects are real but usually minor; the utilization effect is real and usually significant, and it typically points in the opposite, favorable direction.

Secured versus unsecured consolidation loans

Most personal loans used for consolidation are unsecured, meaning no collateral backs the loan and approval is based purely on creditworthiness and income. Some lenders offer secured consolidation options instead, backed by a savings account, a certificate of deposit, or in some cases home equity — and these secured options often come with meaningfully lower rates than an unsecured personal loan would offer the same borrower, because the lender's risk is lower when collateral is on the line.

This lower rate comes with a categorically different risk profile worth understanding clearly before pursuing it: a secured loan converts what was previously unsecured credit card debt —

where the worst-case consequence of non-payment is collections activity and credit damage — into debt backed by a specific asset, where non-payment risks losing that asset directly. A home equity loan or home equity line of credit (HELOC) used to consolidate credit card debt is the starkest version of this tradeoff: a materially lower interest rate, in exchange for converting unsecured debt into debt secured by your home, meaning a sustained inability to pay carries a foreclosure risk that simply didn't exist with the original credit card debt. This isn't a reason to categorically avoid secured consolidation options — for someone with a stable income and a clear-eyed view of the risk, the interest savings can be substantial and genuinely worth it — but it's a decision that deserves more deliberate weighing than the four-question test alone captures, precisely because the downside in a bad-case scenario is qualitatively different, not just quantitatively larger.

Where consolidation offers come from, and why the terms vary so widely

It's worth understanding, briefly, why two consolidation offers on the identical debt profile can look meaningfully different from each other, because the variance isn't random. Consolidation loans are typically underwritten based on credit score, income, existing debt-to-income ratio, and the lender's own risk appetite for a given borrower profile — which means the same $18,000 in card debt might draw an 8% offer from one lender and an 18% offer from another, particularly across the gap between banks, credit unions, and online-only lenders, each of which tends to price risk somewhat differently. Credit unions, in particular, often — though not universally — offer more favorable personal loan rates to members than comparable bank or online offers, partly because of their member-owned, not-for-profit structure; checking a local credit union's consolidation loan terms alongside any mailed offer is a low-effort step worth taking before accepting the first offer that arrives.

A **prequalification check**, offered by most reputable lenders before a full application, typically uses a soft credit inquiry that doesn't affect a credit score, letting you compare real, personalized rate estimates across several lenders before committing to a hard inquiry (which does have a small, temporary credit-score effect) on any single application. Comparing prequalified offers from three or four lenders before choosing one is a standard, low-cost step that a surprising number of people skip, accepting the first offer that lands in their mailbox or inbox instead.

A second worked example: when consolidation is clearly the wrong move

Not every consolidation offer deserves the four-question test's full deliberation — some fail so obviously on the first question that the rest becomes moot. Take a $9,000 balance across two cards, average rate 21%, currently being paid down aggressively at $500 a month under the Chapter 3 order, on track to clear in about 20 months with total interest around $1,650. A consolidation offer arrives: $9,000 personal loan at 14% APR, but structured over a 7-year term with a resulting payment of just $167 a month — a payment that looks dramatically more affordable on paper.

Running question one: total interest on the 7-year, 14% loan comes to roughly $5,000 — more than triple the $1,650 the current aggressive payoff plan would cost. The lower headline rate (14% versus a 21% average) is real, but the extended term more than erases the advantage, because total interest is a function of rate multiplied by time, and seven years at even a lower rate outpaces twenty months at a higher one. This is the term-extension trap from the mechanics section, made concrete: the loan isn't dishonest, and the 14% rate isn't fabricated — the offer is simply structured to look affordable on a monthly basis while costing dramatically more in total, and only running the actual total-interest comparison reveals it. A person evaluating this offer by monthly payment alone, without running question one, would very reasonably conclude it's a good deal. It isn't, and the four-question framework exists specifically to catch offers shaped exactly this way.

Debt management plans: a distinct third option

Separate from a consolidation loan (a new debt that pays off old debts) and a direct settlement negotiation (covered in Chapter 4), a **debt management plan (DMP)**, typically arranged through a nonprofit credit counseling agency such as one accredited by the National Foundation for Credit Counseling, is a structured repayment arrangement where the counseling agency negotiates reduced interest rates directly with your existing creditors — the debts aren't consolidated into a new loan and aren't settled for a reduced balance, but the interest rate on each is lowered, often substantially, and you make a single monthly payment to the counseling agency, which then distributes it to your individual creditors according to the negotiated plan.

This option sits in a genuinely useful middle ground for some situations: it doesn't require taking on new debt the way a consolidation loan does, it doesn't carry the credit-reporting impact of a settlement (payments continue as agreed, generally reported as current rather than settled), and it often achieves a meaningful rate reduction without the borrower needing to negotiate each creditor individually using the Chapter 4 scripts, since the counseling agency typically has established relationships and standard rate-reduction agreements with major card issuers. The tradeoffs: DMPs commonly require closing the enrolled credit accounts as a condition of the reduced rates, typically run over a multi-year term (often three to five years), and may carry a modest monthly administrative fee from the counseling agency, though reputable nonprofit agencies keep this fee low and will disclose it clearly before enrollment. As with any credit counseling arrangement, verifying the agency's nonprofit accreditation before enrolling is a worthwhile, low-effort step — the debt relief space includes both legitimate nonprofit counseling agencies and less scrupulous for-profit operations, and the difference matters.

Chapter 6 — Balance Transfer Mechanics

The situation

A credit card offer arrives: transfer your existing balance to this new card and pay 0% APR for 15 months. For a balance of $5,000 sitting at 22% on an existing card, this looks like an obvious win — over a year of zero interest instead of a rate that's actively working against every payment made. And in a meaningful number of cases, it genuinely is a strong move. But a balance transfer has its own mechanical fine print, and getting the math wrong on it is one of the more common ways people end up worse off despite doing something that looked, on its face, like the responsible choice.

The mechanics

The balance transfer fee is the first number that changes the real math, and it's easy to miss because it's a percentage taken up front rather than an ongoing rate. Typically in the range of 3-5% of the transferred balance, charged at the time of transfer and added to the new card's balance, this fee is the real cost of the 0% period — not zero, as the marketing implies, but a one-time cost that needs to be weighed against the interest it's replacing.

The promotional period's fixed length is the second mechanical detail, and it matters because whatever balance remains unpaid when the promotional period ends typically reverts to a standard purchase or penalty APR — often significantly higher than the rate on the card you transferred away from in the first place. A balance transfer used as a genuine payoff accelerant, with a real plan to clear the balance before the promotional window closes, is a fundamentally different tool than a balance transfer used to defer a problem, with no realistic plan to pay it off before the standard rate resets and compounds against a now-larger balance (larger because of the fee added at transfer).

The break-even calculation ties these two pieces together into the single number that actually determines whether a given transfer offer is worth taking: does the fee cost less than the interest it saves, given a realistic payoff timeline? This is calculable with basic arithmetic and should be run before accepting any transfer offer, not estimated by feel.

A less obvious mechanical detail: **most balance transfer promotions do not apply to new purchases made on the same card**, only to the transferred balance itself. Using a balance transfer card for everyday spending during the promotional period, while carrying a transferred balance, often means new purchases accrue interest at the card's standard rate from the moment they post — even while the transferred balance sits at 0% — because payments are frequently applied to the lowest-interest balance first under standard card-issuer payment allocation rules, leaving the higher-rate new purchases to accrue interest unchecked. Treating a balance transfer card as a payoff tool only, not a spending card, avoids this trap entirely.

The framework

A three-step process for evaluating any balance transfer offer:

Step one: calculate the transfer fee in real dollars. Multiply the balance you'd transfer by the fee percentage. This is the guaranteed, immediate cost of the move.

Step two: calculate the interest you'd actually pay on the current card if you didn't transfer, over the same number of months as the new card's promotional period, using your realistic payoff payment amount. This is the cost you're trying to avoid.

Step three: compare the two. If the transfer fee is meaningfully smaller than the interest it would replace, the transfer is a clear win, assuming a realistic plan exists to pay off the balance before the promotional period ends. If the fee and the avoided interest are close, or if the realistic payoff timeline extends past the promotional period (meaning the remaining balance will revert to a standard, often elevated, rate), the transfer's advantage shrinks or disappears, and it may not be worth the account inquiry, the new account opening (which can have a minor, temporary effect on credit history), and the administrative complexity.

A hard rule to pair with the calculation: divide the transferred balance by the number of months in the promotional period, and set that amount as the fixed minimum monthly target — not the card's actual minimum payment, which will typically be far smaller and will not clear the balance before the promotional rate expires. Treat that self-set target as non-negotiable for the life of the promotional period.

The worked example

A $5,000 balance currently at 22% APR, offered a transfer to a new card with 0% APR for 15 months and a 3% transfer fee.

Step one: transfer fee is $150 (3% of $5,000).

Step two: paying down $5,000 at 22% APR over 15 months, at a fixed payment that clears the balance in that window, requires a monthly payment of roughly $370, and the total interest paid over those 15 months on the original card comes to approximately $555.

Step three: comparing the $150 fee against the $555 in avoided interest, the transfer saves roughly $405 — a real, meaningful savings — provided the full balance is paid off within the 15-month window at the required $370-ish monthly target (in this case, $5,150 including the fee, divided across 15 months, comes to about $343 a month as the fixed target).

Now the counter-case, using the same $5,000 balance but a realistic monthly payment capacity of only $200 rather than $370. At $200 a month, the balance won't clear within the 15-month window — roughly $2,000 will remain when the promotional period ends, at which point it typically reverts to a standard rate that could run 20% or higher. In this version, the transfer still saves real interest during the promotional months themselves, but the person needs to go into the decision knowing explicitly that a balance will remain at the 15-month mark, with a plan for what happens to it — a second transfer to another 0% offer if one's available and the timing works, an accelerated payment push in the final months before expiration, or an honest acceptance that the standard rate will apply to whatever's left. The transfer isn't a bad move at $200 a month; it's a genuinely useful tool that still needs an explicit exit plan for the leftover balance, the same discipline required of the consolidation loan in Chapter 5. The math never fails on its own. What fails is treating either tool as a complete solution instead of one accelerant that still needs the payoff order from Chapter 3 running underneath it the entire time.

Employer and community-based debt assistance programs

Beyond the creditor-facing negotiation tools covered in Chapter 4 and the consolidation and transfer tools covered in this chapter and the last, a range of employer and community-based programs exist that many people carrying debt never think to check. Some employers, particularly larger organizations, offer financial wellness benefits — sometimes including access to low-cost or no-cost financial counseling, occasionally even a small employer-matched debt-payoff or student-loan-repayment benefit — bundled into a broader benefits package and easy to overlook entirely if it isn't mentioned during onboarding. It's worth checking your own employer's benefits documentation, or asking HR directly, specifically about financial wellness or student loan assistance programs, since these benefits are frequently underused simply because they're not well advertised relative to more visible benefits like health insurance or retirement matching.

Community-based resources are similarly worth a direct check rather than an assumption they don't apply: local nonprofit credit counseling agencies (the NFCC-accredited organizations mentioned in this book's Notes section), community action agencies, and in some cases religious or civic organizations maintain emergency assistance funds specifically for utility, medical, or housing-related debt for community members facing acute hardship. These resources vary enormously by location and aren't a substitute for the systematic frameworks built throughout this book, but for a debt load that includes a genuine hardship-driven balance — a large unexpected medical bill, a utility arrearage during a job loss — checking whether a local assistance program exists before defaulting straight to a credit-based solution is a worthwhile, low-cost step, and one that's easy to skip simply because it doesn't occur to most people to look.

Introductory rate offers on new purchases versus balance transfers: reading the fine print correctly

Some cards advertise a promotional 0% rate on both balance transfers and new purchases simultaneously, sometimes at the same rate and for the same duration, sometimes with different terms for each. It's worth reading these two provisions as entirely separate promises rather than assuming they behave identically, since issuers are not required to structure them the same way, and a surprising number of cardholders discover the distinction only after a payment allocation didn't work the way they expected.

Where a card offers different promotional terms for purchases and transfers — a common structure — payment allocation rules typically apply any payment above the required minimum to the balance with the lowest promotional or standard rate first, under federal regulations governing card issuer payment application (a protection specifically enacted following past practices where issuers could apply payments to the lowest-rate balance regardless of cardholder preference, precisely the kind of practice that made this rule necessary). This matters directly for the "transfer card as payoff tool only" recommendation made earlier in this chapter: if a 0% purchase rate and a 0% transfer rate are running concurrently, spending on that card doesn't create the interest-accrual risk described earlier, since both balances remain at 0% simultaneously — but the moment either promotional window ends while the other is still active, the same payment-allocation dynamics apply, and it's worth re-checking the specific terms for your card the moment any part of a multi-rate promotional structure changes, rather than assuming the original terms still describe the account's current behavior.

Balance transfers and credit utilization: a short-term side effect

Opening a new balance transfer card increases total available revolving credit immediately, which — independent of the transferred balance itself — can produce a short-term improvement in overall credit utilization (the ratio of total revolving balances to total available revolving credit, a meaningful factor in most credit scoring models), simply because the denominator of that ratio grew even before any payment has been made. This is a real, if secondary, byproduct, separate from the interest-savings calculation that's the primary reason to consider a transfer in the first place.

It comes with an equally real caution, and it's the same caution that ran through Chapter 5's consolidation discussion: newly available credit — whether from a new balance transfer card's available limit beyond the transferred amount, or from an old card left open after its balance moves elsewhere — is only a neutral or positive development if it isn't used to accumulate new balances alongside the one being actively paid down. The utilization benefit of a balance transfer is real and immediate; it is also easily and quickly erased by new spending on either the new or the old card, which is precisely why this chapter's mechanics section recommended treating a transfer card as a payoff tool only, not a spending card, for the duration of the promotional period.

Deferred interest versus 0% APR: never confuse the two

A related but structurally different offer worth distinguishing clearly from the 0% APR balance transfer covered throughout this chapter is **deferred interest financing**, commonly seen on retail store financing for larger purchases (furniture, electronics, appliances) rather than on balance transfers specifically. The two look similar on the surface — both advertise "no interest" for a set promotional period — but they behave very differently if the balance isn't cleared in full by the deadline.

Under a true 0% APR offer, interest simply begins accruing at the standard rate, going forward, on whatever balance remains after the promotional period ends — the months already elapsed under the 0% rate stay interest-free regardless of what happens afterward. Under deferred interest financing, by contrast, if the full balance isn't paid off by the end of the promotional period, interest is often charged retroactively, back to the original purchase date, on the entire original balance — not just the remaining amount, and not just from the deadline forward. This is a materially worse outcome for a balance that narrowly misses the deadline, and it's a distinction that's easy to miss because the marketing language for both types of offer often sounds identical ("no interest for 12 months"). Before assuming any 0%-labeled offer behaves like the balance transfer mechanics described earlier in this chapter, check explicitly whether the specific offer's terms describe true 0% APR or deferred interest — the fine print will state it explicitly, and the difference, in a worst-case scenario, can be the entire promotional period's interest charged in a single retroactive lump sum rather than just the interest on the remaining balance going forward.

Sequential balance transfers: a real tool, with a real limit

Some people, particularly those carrying larger balances that can't realistically clear within a single 15-18 month promotional window even at an aggressive payment, use a strategy of sequential balance transfers — moving a remaining balance to a new 0% offer again once the first promotional period is ending, and repeating as needed. This is a legitimate, real strategy, used successfully by plenty of people managing larger balances over a longer horizon, but it carries real risks, stated directly rather than treating it as a costless way to defer a balance indefinitely.

Each new transfer typically incurs another transfer fee (the 3-5% range from earlier in this chapter, applied again to whatever balance remains), which erodes the interest savings each time it's repeated — a balance transferred three times over several years pays the fee three times, and at some point the cumulative fees can approach or exceed what a straightforward, non-transferred payoff at a moderate fixed rate would have cost. Approval for a new promotional offer is also never guaranteed — issuers can and do tighten approval criteria, and a credit profile that qualified for the first transfer may not automatically qualify for a second or third, especially if several new account inquiries have accumulated on the credit report from the transfers themselves. And each new account opened resets certain credit-history factors, however modestly, which can have a small compounding effect on credit standing across several sequential openings in a short period.

None of this makes sequential transfers a bad strategy categorically — for a genuinely large balance with no realistic single-window payoff plan, it can still beat carrying the balance at a standard rate the entire time. But it should be treated as a deliberate, calculated strategy with a real ceiling on how many times it's worth repeating, not a default assumption that a fresh 0% offer will always be available on demand whenever the current one runs low.

Qualifying for the best offers, and what to do if you don't

The most attractive balance transfer offers — the longest 0% windows, the lowest transfer fees — are typically reserved for applicants with strong credit profiles, and it's worth being honest about this up front rather than discovering it after applying and receiving a weaker offer than expected, which also results in a hard credit inquiry that was spent on an offer you didn't end up using. If your credit profile is closer to fair than excellent, check prequalification tools (which, like the consolidation loan prequalification mentioned in Chapter 5, typically use a soft inquiry that doesn't affect your score) before applying outright, to get a realistic sense of what promotional terms you're likely to actually receive.

Not every card issuer, either, allows a balance transfer from another card issued by the same parent company — a restriction that catches people off guard when the "new" card they're offered turns out to be issued by the same bank as the card they're trying to move a balance away from. Confirm this specific detail before applying if you're transferring away from a major bank's card, since applying for an offer you're structurally ineligible for wastes a credit inquiry for nothing.

What happens if you can't make the fixed target payment some month

Life happens during a promotional period the same way it happens during any other stretch of a payoff plan, and it's worth having an explicit answer ready for the month a car repair or a reduced paycheck makes the fixed target payment from this chapter's framework impossible to hit. The mechanically correct response, in order: first, pay whatever you can above the card's actual minimum, even if it's below the calculated target — any amount above the minimum still reduces principal and still helps, even if it slips the payoff outside the promotional window by a month or two. Second, recalculate the remaining balance against the remaining promotional months immediately after the shortfall, rather than waiting until the period is nearly over to notice the timeline has shifted — an early recalculation gives you more months to make up the gap with smaller adjustments; a late one forces a much larger catch-up payment or an acceptance that some balance will carry into the standard rate. Third, if it becomes clear well in advance that the full balance won't clear in time, start researching a second transfer offer or a Chapter 5 consolidation option for the remaining balance before the promotional rate resets, rather than after — every week a decision gets made ahead of a rate change instead of in reaction to one is a week of additional options still on the table.

Chapter 7 — The Motivation Question: Which Order Actually Finishes

The situation

Two people, each carrying five debts, each with the same total balance and the same extra monthly payment available, both run the math from Chapter 2 and both get the same result: the avalanche order saves roughly $1,800 more than the snowball order. One follows the avalanche order exactly as calculated. The other, after reading the math, deliberately chooses the hybrid order from Chapter 3, accepting a smaller, calculated cost in exchange for an earlier full payoff. Eighteen months later, one of them is still on track, and the other has stopped making extra payments entirely, back to minimums, debt largely where it was eight months earlier. The math didn't fail either person. Something else did, and it's worth addressing directly, tactically, without turning it into a chapter about willpower or a personality trait.

The mechanics

This is the one chapter in this book that touches something psychology-adjacent, and it's worth being precise about the difference between what this chapter does and what a book about the psychology of debt would do. A psychological treatment would ask why a person accumulates debt, what unconscious pattern the spending serves, what a specific number means to a specific person's sense of self. That's real, valuable territory, and it's simply not this chapter's job. This chapter asks a narrower, purely tactical question: given that a payoff plan requires sustained action over months or years, which structural features of a plan make sustained action more likely, regardless of who's running the plan or why they got into debt in the first place?

There's a real, non-fabricated finding worth citing directly here, because it's the closest thing to hard evidence this specific question has: a study published in the *Journal of Marketing Research* (Gal and McShane, 2012), using account-level data obtained from a debt settlement firm, found that closing individual debt accounts entirely — regardless of the dollar balance of those accounts — predicted overall debt elimination, while the dollar size of the closed accounts did not predict it once the number of accounts closed was accounted for. In practical terms, the researchers found that people carrying multiple credit card balances were more likely to eliminate their total debt when they focused first on paying off the smallest balances — the snowball approach — even though it isn't the mathematically optimal order. The researchers' interpretation centered on the value of an early, complete "win" as a driver of continued follow-through, more than on the specific dollar amount saved along the way. This finding gets cited constantly by proponents of the snowball method, and it deserves to be — but it's worth being precise about what it does and doesn't establish. It's one study, using one dataset, examining one behavioral pattern; it's not a universal law, and it doesn't mean the avalanche method is destined to fail for any given individual. What it does establish, credibly, is that "which order produces a real, complete win soonest" is a legitimate variable worth weighing alongside "which order is mathematically optimal" — not a lesser, softer consideration to be waved off in favor of pure arithmetic.

Underneath that finding sits a mechanical explanation worth understanding on its own terms, independent of the study: a payoff plan is a long chain of identical-feeling months with very little externally visible change, especially under a pure avalanche order applied to a large, high-rate debt that takes a long time to move. Humans, in general, sustain effortful behavior more easily when the behavior produces periodic, concrete evidence that it's working — this is a widely observed pattern in behavior-change research generally, not specific to debt, and it shows up in everything from exercise habits to savings goals. A payoff order that front-loads at least one complete, bankable win produces that evidence early. A payoff order that doesn't produce a single complete payoff for a year or more asks a person to sustain motivation purely on faith in a spreadsheet, for a long stretch, with no concrete milestone to point to.

None of this means the snowball method is correct and the avalanche method is wrong. It means the honest tactical answer depends on a real, answerable question about the specific person running the plan: how many total debts are there, how long would the avalanche order realistically take to produce its first complete payoff, and how confident is that person, honestly, in their own ability to sustain a plan with no complete win for that long. That's not a soft or unmeasurable question — it has a concrete answer for any given set of debts, and the hybrid method from Chapter 3 exists precisely because most real situations don't require choosing one philosophy in its pure form.

The framework

A three-question tactical assessment, to be run honestly rather than optimistically:

Question one: under the pure avalanche order, how many months until the first complete debt payoff? Calculate this directly from your simulation in Chapter 2. If the answer is under four to six months, the pure avalanche order likely delivers an early win on its own timeline and there's little reason to deviate from it.

Question two: have you previously abandoned a financial plan (a budget, a savings goal, a previous payoff attempt) before completion? This is not a character judgment — it's a data point about your own track record with sustained, low-feedback effort, and it should be weighed honestly rather than defensively. A "yes" here is a legitimate reason to weight the plan toward earlier wins, not a personal failing to feel bad about.

Question three: is the dollar gap between avalanche and hybrid, calculated in Chapter 2 and Chapter 3, small relative to your total debt (roughly under 5-10% of total interest) or large (well above that)? A small gap makes the hybrid method's tradeoff easy to justify regardless of your answers to questions one and two. A large gap raises the stakes of the choice and deserves more honest self-assessment before deciding to sacrifice it for an earlier win.

The decision rule that follows: if question one's answer is already short, stick with pure avalanche — you're getting both the optimal math and an early win without needing to trade anything. If question one's answer is long (a year or more to first payoff) and question two's answer is yes, shift meaningfully toward the hybrid or even a closer-to-pure-snowball order, because the real, calculable cost of doing so is very likely smaller than the real, calculable cost of abandoning a plan with no wins in it at all — a completed hybrid plan beats an abandoned optimal one, every time, by definition. If question three's gap is large, look for a middle path specifically: the hybrid method's threshold-based approach (Chapter 3) rather than a full switch to pure snowball, since it preserves most of the avalanche's savings while still manufacturing an early complete payoff.

A separate, purely mechanical motivation tool, usable regardless of which order you choose: track and visibly display total-debt-remaining as a single number, updated monthly, rather than tracking each account separately. A single combined number that moves down consistently, even while individual accounts remain open and unchanged, produces more of the "visible progress" effect than watching five separate, mostly-static account balances — because the combined number moves every single month, from every single payment, regardless of which specific account absorbed the extra payment that month.

The worked example

Someone with six debts totaling $34,000, running a pure avalanche simulation, finds the first complete payoff (a small personal loan that happens to also carry a mid-range rate) doesn't land until month fourteen. She's abandoned two prior budgeting attempts in the past three years, both times around the six-to-eight-month mark, once a period of good progress without any complete milestone started to feel like it wasn't going anywhere.

Running the three-question assessment: question one comes back long (fourteen months to first win). Question two comes back yes (two prior abandoned attempts). Question three — she calculates the gap between full avalanche and the hybrid order at roughly $340 in extra interest, against a total debt of $34,000, well under the 5-10% threshold that would make the tradeoff costly.

The decision rule points clearly toward the hybrid method. She reorders her debts to clear a small $580 balance first (used to be ranked fourth under pure avalanche), producing a complete payoff at month two instead of month fourteen, at a calculated cost of roughly $340 in additional interest over the life of the full plan — about 1% of her total debt. Twelve months earlier than the pure avalanche schedule would have delivered any complete win, she has a closed account, a combined-debt tracker that's visibly moved, and — measured against her actual history of abandoning plans around month six to eight — a real structural reason to believe this attempt clears that mark differently than the previous two did. The $340 isn't a cost paid for comfort. It's a calculated, deliberate insurance premium against a documented, personal risk of abandonment, priced at roughly 1% of the total debt being resolved — which, measured against the alternative of a plan that stalls out again at month seven with the debt still substantially intact, is a genuinely cheap trade.

Structural features besides balance size that produce the same effect

The small-balance-first logic behind the snowball method is really a specific case of a broader tactical principle: any structural feature of a payoff order that produces visible, bankable progress on a predictable cadence tends to support sustained follow-through better than an order that doesn't, and balance size is simply the easiest such feature to build a rule around. A few other structural features worth considering, usable alongside or instead of a pure balance-size rule depending on what's true of your specific debts.

Account-count reduction as its own tracked metric — the number of open, unpaid accounts remaining — sometimes produces a stronger visible-progress effect than dollar balance alone, particularly for someone carrying many small accounts rather than a few large ones. Watching "6 open accounts" become "5, then 4, then 3" can register as more tangible progress than watching a large combined dollar total decline gradually, even when the underlying dollar progress is identical either way. For a debt profile with many small accounts (several store cards, a mix of buy-now-pay-later balances, a couple of medical bills), weighting the payoff order toward clearing whole accounts quickly — which the small-balance rule already tends to do as a side effect — can be treated as a deliberate goal in its own right, not just an incidental byproduct.

Choosing the small-balance threshold deliberately, not by default

Chapter 3 recommended a default small-balance threshold — a debt that would clear within roughly one to three months at your extra-payment amount — without spending much time on why that specific range, rather than a longer or shorter window, is the right default. It's worth revisiting here, in more depth, because the threshold you choose is the single most consequential number in the entire hybrid framework, and it's worth setting deliberately rather than accepting the default without understanding what it's trading off.

A shorter threshold (say, clearing within one month only) minimizes the interest cost of the quick-win adjustment to nearly nothing, but it also captures fewer debts under the early-win rule, meaning fewer situations actually get an accelerated first payoff worth mentioning. A longer threshold (say, up to six months) captures more debts under the quick-win rule, producing more opportunities for an early complete payoff across a larger, more varied debt portfolio, but it also concedes more real interest savings relative to a pure avalanche order, since a debt held at the front of the line for up to six months, rather than one to three, has correspondingly more time to represent foregone avalanche-optimal sequencing on the higher-rate debts sitting behind it.

There's no single correct threshold for every situation — it's a genuine tradeoff, and the right setting depends on the same factors Chapter 7 asks you to assess explicitly: how much of an early win do you realistically need to sustain the plan, and how large is the dollar cost of extending the threshold for your specific set of balances and rates. For most portfolios, the one-to-three-month default strikes a reasonable balance and rarely needs adjustment. For a portfolio with a demonstrated high risk of abandonment (Chapter 7's honest self-assessment) and a small rate spread across debts (meaning the avalanche's overall advantage is modest to begin with, as covered in Chapter 2), extending the threshold further is a defensible, calculated choice rather than a compromise made carelessly.

A practical routine for staying with the plan month to month

Beyond the structural choice of payoff order, a handful of simple, repeatable habits materially improve the odds of a plan surviving to completion, and they're worth listing plainly because they're the kind of thing that seems too obvious to mention and gets skipped for exactly that reason.

A fixed monthly review date, calendared in advance, on which every debt balance gets updated, the combined-total tracker gets refreshed, and the next month's extra payment gets confirmed and scheduled. Treating this as a recurring, non-optional appointment — the same way a bill's due date is non-optional — removes the plan from the category of "something I mean to check on periodically" and moves it into the category of "something that happens automatically, on a fixed schedule, regardless of how busy or distracted the surrounding month has been."

Automating the minimum payments on every debt, even the ones not currently receiving extra payment, removes the single most common source of an accidental missed payment (covered in Chapter 10's mistake list) — a payment simply forgotten during a busy stretch, on an account that wasn't top of mind because it wasn't the current focus of the plan.

Keeping the extra payment itself manual rather than automated, at least during the active build-up phase of a payoff plan, is a deliberate exception to the automation principle above, worth explaining directly: a manual extra payment, made consciously each month, keeps the plan's progress genuinely visible and felt, in a way that a fully automated extra payment — set once and forgotten — doesn't. This is a minor, optional refinement rather than a hard rule, and some people do prefer full automation for the reduced friction it offers; the tradeoff matters either way, since it connects directly to the visible-progress mechanism this chapter has spent most of its length establishing.

Milestone framing on a single large debt, for someone whose portfolio doesn't have several small accounts to clear early but does have one large one, is a workable substitute: rather than waiting for a full account closure as the only visible marker, set explicit sub-milestones on the large balance itself — every $1,000 or $2,500 cleared, marked and acknowledged deliberately, even though the account itself remains open. This doesn't produce the exact same effect as a genuine account closure (there's a real difference between "still open, but smaller" and "closed"), but it's a legitimate way to manufacture some of the same visible-progress benefit within a payoff order that, for good financial reasons, keeps a single large high-rate debt as the priority target throughout.

What the research doesn't say, and where the line actually is

It's worth being precise about a distinction this chapter has referenced but not yet stated outright, because overclaiming a real finding is exactly the kind of error a book like this one exists to avoid. The Gal and McShane research, cited earlier in this chapter, examined actual account-level repayment data and found a correlation between small-balance-first repayment and overall debt elimination — it did not, and does not claim to, establish that every person, in every situation, does better on a pure snowball order than a pure avalanche order. A correlation observed across a large dataset describes a general tendency, not a guarantee about any specific individual's outcome. Someone with strong follow-through on long, low-feedback plans — evidenced honestly by question two in the framework above —

may do just as well, or better in total dollar terms, on a pure avalanche order, and the research doesn't argue otherwise.

What the finding does support, credibly, is the structural logic underneath this chapter's framework: an early, complete win is a real, measurable lever on follow-through, worth weighing deliberately rather than dismissing as a soft or unserious consideration next to "the math." That's a materially different, more defensible claim than "everyone should use the snowball method," and it's the claim this book is actually making.

A note on plans that fail even with an early win built in

Building an early win into the payoff order improves the odds of follow-through — it doesn't guarantee it. If a plan stalls out despite a well-designed hybrid order, the honest next step isn't to conclude the framework failed; it's to look for a cause outside the payoff-order mechanics entirely — a genuine change in income or expenses that's made the extra-payment amount itself unrealistic, a life event that's consumed bandwidth no payoff order was ever going to account for, or simply a case where the original extra-payment number was set too optimistically from the start. Revisit the actual monthly extra-payment figure honestly before revisiting the order again; a hybrid order built around an unrealistic $600-a-month extra payment will stall regardless of how well the sequencing was designed, and the fix in that case is a smaller, more sustainable extra-payment number run through the same framework, not an abandonment of the plan altogether.

Accountability structures, evaluated tactically rather than as a given

A common piece of general debt-payoff advice is to "tell someone" or "find an accountability partner," offered so often and so generically that it's worth examining tactically rather than accepting on faith, the same way this book examines every other piece of common advice. The mechanism behind why this sometimes helps is straightforward: a plan that's only visible to the person running it can quietly bend or pause without any external friction, while a plan that's visible to at least one other person adds a small but real social cost to abandoning it, functioning similarly to the visible-progress principle covered earlier in this chapter, just sourced externally rather than from the plan's own structure.

This isn't universally necessary — someone who scores well on question two's honest self-assessment (a strong track record of finishing long, low-feedback plans) may get little additional benefit from external accountability, since the internal structure is already sufficient. But for someone whose honest answer to question two is closer to "no, I've stalled before," pairing the hybrid payoff order with a specific, low-friction accountability structure — sharing the combined-debt tracker number with one trusted person on a fixed monthly cadence, for instance, rather than a vague general intention to "check in sometime" — is a legitimate, low-cost addition to the plan, evaluated the same way every other tool in this book is evaluated: by what it actually does mechanically, not by whether it sounds virtuous.

When to revisit the chosen order entirely

Most of this chapter has focused on sustaining a chosen order once it's built. Briefly, here are the handful of situations that genuinely warrant rebuilding the order from scratch rather than simply continuing: a material, sustained change in monthly extra-payment capacity (a raise, a job loss, a major new fixed expense) that changes the realistic timeline meaningfully; a new debt added to the portfolio that wasn't part of the original calculation; or — the situation this chapter exists to address directly — a demonstrated pattern of stalling under the current order that a shift toward more front-loaded wins would plausibly fix. Absent one of these three triggers, the better move is almost always to continue executing the order already built rather than repeatedly re-optimizing it; a payoff order re-evaluated every few weeks on no new information is itself a form of the structural instability this chapter is trying to help you avoid, just wearing analytical clothing instead of avoidance.

Chapter 8 — Handling Multiple Debt Types at Once

The situation

A payoff order built purely on interest rate works cleanly when every debt is the same kind of thing — five credit cards, all revolving, all behaving the same way. Real debt loads are rarely that clean. A more typical mix looks like: $14,000 in federal student loans at a blended rate around 5.5%, a $22,000 auto loan at 7%, $3,000 in medical debt at 0% on a hospital payment plan, and $6,500 across two credit cards averaging 23%. The pure interest-rate sort says pay the credit cards first, and on pure math, it's right — but student loans, auto loans, and medical debt each carry structural features that the simple rate comparison doesn't capture, and ignoring those features can lead to a technically-optimal-looking plan that creates real problems elsewhere.

The mechanics

Federal student loans carry protections no other common debt type has: income-driven repayment plans that cap monthly payments as a percentage of income, deferment and forbearance options during hardship, and loan forgiveness programs for specific careers or circumstances (public service, for instance) that, where applicable, can eliminate remaining balances entirely after a qualifying period. These protections are valuable independent of the interest rate, and they're the reason federal student loans are usually the wrong candidate for aggressive extra payments or consolidation into a private loan, even when their rate isn't the lowest in the portfolio — the protections themselves function as a form of insurance that a slightly lower rate elsewhere doesn't replace. Private student loans carry none of these federal protections regardless of who services them, and should generally be treated like any other high-rate installment debt in the payoff order — sorted by actual rate, with no special deference.

Auto loans are secured debt — the vehicle itself is collateral, and default carries a consequence no unsecured debt does: repossession. This changes the priority calculus in one specific way regardless of the interest rate: an auto loan payment should never be the one sacrificed to free up cash for extra payments elsewhere, because falling behind risks losing an asset that, in most households, is also required for earning the income that's funding the entire payoff plan in the first place. Beyond making the minimum payment a non-negotiable floor, auto loans should otherwise be sorted into the standard rate-based order like any other installment debt.

Medical debt carries several structural quirks. It's frequently interest-free or low-interest when arranged directly with a provider or hospital billing department (as opposed to already sold to a collector), and providers are often willing to negotiate the total balance down directly — sometimes substantially — particularly for uninsured or underinsured patients, using the same leverage logic covered in Chapter 4: ask, in writing if possible, about financial assistance or charity care programs, which many hospitals (particularly nonprofit hospitals, which often have specific policies tied to their tax-exempt status) are required to offer and don't always advertise clearly. Medical debt also has some specific credit-reporting protections that have shifted over recent years — verify current credit-reporting treatment for medical debt directly with the credit bureaus or a nonprofit credit counselor, since these rules are one of the more frequently updated areas of consumer credit policy and any specific number stated here would risk going stale.

Credit card and other unsecured revolving debt is, generally, the least protected and typically the highest-rate category, which is exactly why it dominates the rate-based sort in most real portfolios — there's rarely a structural reason to deviate from pure rate-order on this category alone.

The framework

A modified sorting rule for mixed debt types, layered on top of the Chapter 3 hybrid framework:

Step one: segment debts by type first — federal student loans, private student loans and other unsecured installment debt, secured debt (auto, and any other collateralized loan), and medical/hospital debt.

Step two: remove federal student loans from the aggressive-payoff pool entirely, unless a specific, verified reason applies (a rate so high it exceeds every other debt significantly, or a documented decision to forgo a forgiveness program you don't expect to qualify for). Keep federal student loans on their standard repayment schedule, potentially on an income-driven plan if that reduces required cash flow, and redirect the freed-up capacity toward the rest of the portfolio.

Step three: treat the secured-debt minimum as untouchable, not just low-priority. The auto loan minimum gets paid before anything else in the entire budget, full stop, ahead of even the highest-rate credit card, because the consequence of missing it (repossession) is categorically worse than the cost of one more month of high-rate credit card interest.

Step four: attempt direct negotiation on any medical debt before including it in the rate-sorted order at all — a successfully negotiated reduction changes the balance itself, which should happen before that balance gets slotted into the payoff sequence, not after.

Step five: run the remaining debts — private student loans, unsecured installment loans, credit cards, and any negotiated-down medical balance — through the standard

Chapter 3 hybrid sort, exactly as if they were the only debts in the picture.

The worked example

Back to the mixed portfolio: $14,000 federal student loans (5.5%), $22,000 auto loan (7%), $3,000 medical debt (0%, hospital plan), $6,500 across two credit cards (23% average). Extra payment available: $450 a month.

Step two removes the $14,000 in federal loans from the aggressive pool — they stay on standard repayment, protections intact, at whatever minimum the servicer requires.

Step three locks the auto loan's minimum as untouchable, but the auto loan itself, beyond its minimum, still competes in the rate-sorted order at 7% — it's just guaranteed its minimum payment regardless of where it ranks.

Step four: a call to the hospital billing department, using the Chapter 4 script adapted for a medical context, results in the $3,000 medical debt being reduced to $2,100 through a documented financial-hardship discount program the hospital offers but doesn't list on its billing statements.

Step five sorts what remains — the $6,500 in credit cards at 23%, the $2,100 negotiated medical balance at 0%, and the $22,000 auto loan at 7% (beyond its guaranteed minimum) — through the hybrid framework. The medical balance, being both small and 0%, gets minimum-only treatment per the zero-interest exception from Chapter 3, unless it's small enough to qualify for the small-balance quick-win rule, in which case it moves to the front purely for the early win despite costing nothing to accelerate. The $6,500 in credit cards, being both the highest rate and, split across two cards, likely to include at least one balance small enough to clear quickly, becomes the primary target for the $450 in extra monthly payments. The auto loan, at 7%, sits last in the extra-payment queue but continues receiving its full minimum throughout, protected regardless of its position.

The resulting plan looks meaningfully different from a naive pure-rate sort across all four debts combined, and it's a better plan for it — not because it saves marginally more money (it doesn't, materially), but because it correctly treats four structurally different debts as four structurally different problems, each with its own right answer, layered underneath the same payoff-order logic running the whole time.

A closer look at income-driven repayment for federal student loans

Because federal student loans are held out of the aggressive-payoff pool in most cases, it's worth understanding the mechanism that makes that decision correct rather than simply accepting it on faith. Income-driven repayment (IDR) plans calculate a required monthly payment as a percentage of discretionary income, generally recalculated annually based on updated income and family size, rather than as a fixed amortization schedule tied purely to the loan balance and a standard term. This structure means a genuine drop in income — a job loss, a reduction in hours, a return to school — automatically reduces the required payment, sometimes to very little or even zero, without the loan going delinquent, and without the account being reported as missed or late, provided the required paperwork is filed on time.

This is a categorically different kind of protection than anything available on a private loan, a credit card, or an auto loan, all of which require a proactive hardship request (Chapter 4) that may or may not be granted, rather than a built-in, automatic adjustment. Weighed against this, a federal loan's interest rate — even one that isn't the lowest in a given portfolio — is often still the wrong candidate for redirected extra payments, because the protection itself has a real value that doesn't show up anywhere in a simple rate comparison. The plain exception: someone with high, stable income and no realistic scenario in which they'd need income-driven flexibility, holding a federal loan at a rate that's genuinely higher than every other debt in their portfolio, may reasonably choose to prioritize it on pure rate grounds — the framework in this chapter is a strong default, not an absolute rule for every circumstance.

Medical debt: negotiating before it reaches collections

The negotiation window on medical debt is meaningfully wider before an account is sent to collections than after, and it's worth acting inside that window deliberately rather than letting a bill sit unaddressed until a collector calls. Most hospitals and many other healthcare providers have a financial assistance or charity care policy — often required by law for nonprofit hospitals seeking to maintain their tax-exempt status — that can reduce or, for qualifying income levels, entirely eliminate a balance. These policies are rarely surfaced automatically; they typically require a direct request, sometimes an application with income documentation, made to the hospital's billing or financial counseling department specifically, not the general customer service line.

A workable script for this specific call: "I've received a bill for [amount] and I'm not able to pay it in full. Can you tell me about any financial assistance, charity care, or hardship discount programs the hospital offers, and how I'd apply?" This framing — asking about a named program rather than simply asking for a lower bill — tends to route the call to someone with actual authority to discuss the relevant policy, rather than a general billing representative who may not proactively mention it. If a first call doesn't surface a program, asking directly whether the provider offers an uninsured or self-pay discount (a separate, often more automatic, discount some providers apply regardless of income, simply for paying without going through insurance) is worth a second, specific attempt before assuming no room exists.

A note on debt collection agencies specific to medical and student loan debt

Both medical debt and student loan debt, once delinquent, can be assigned to collection agencies that specialize specifically in those debt types, and some of the general collections mechanics from Chapter 4 apply with modifications specific to each. Medical debt collectors are still bound by the FDCPA the same as any other consumer debt collector, and the same validation-request and negotiation approach from Chapter 4 applies directly — with the added step, covered earlier in this chapter, of checking for a billing error or an unexhausted financial assistance program before treating the collections balance as a fixed, final number to negotiate down from.

Federal student loan default is handled through a different mechanism entirely, worth distinguishing clearly from private-collections dynamics: the Department of Education (or its assigned servicers and, in some cases, the Treasury Department for federal offset actions) has collection powers beyond what a typical private collector holds, including the ability to garnish wages or offset federal tax refunds without first obtaining a court judgment, under authority specific to federal student debt. This is precisely why the earlier sections of this chapter treat catching a federal student loan default before it happens — through income-driven repayment enrollment, deferment, or forbearance — as categorically more urgent than a comparable private debt default, where the standard court-judgment process from Chapter 4's lawsuit discussion would typically apply instead.

Medical debt, insurance disputes, and the billing-error angle

A meaningful share of medical debt, distinct from the financial-hardship negotiation covered earlier in this chapter, stems from billing errors or insurance processing issues rather than a genuine, correctly calculated balance — a claim submitted with an incorrect billing code, a service that should have been covered under an insurance plan but was processed as out-of-network or denied in error, or a bill generated before an insurance payment was fully applied. This is worth checking before entering a hardship negotiation on any medical bill of meaningful size, since a billing error, once identified and corrected, can reduce or eliminate a balance more completely than any negotiated discount would.

A practical first step: request an itemized bill (distinct from the summary statement typically sent first) from the provider's billing department, and compare it line by line against the insurance company's Explanation of Benefits (EOB) for the same service, checking specifically for services billed that weren't actually received, duplicate charges, or a mismatch between what the provider billed and what the EOB shows as the correct patient responsibility. Discrepancies of this kind are common enough in medical billing that this comparison is worth making a standard step before any medical debt gets negotiated or paid, not just for large balances — a billing-error dispute resolved directly with the provider or the insurer, using their own formal appeals or billing-dispute process, is a genuinely different and often more complete resolution than a hardship discount negotiated on a balance that may have been calculated incorrectly to begin with.

Coordinating multiple household members' debt

A detail this chapter hasn't yet addressed directly: many of the mixed-debt-type situations this chapter covers occur within a household carrying debt across more than one person — a couple with individual and joint accounts, for instance. The mechanics in this chapter and throughout the book apply identically regardless of whose name is on which account, but coordination adds a real, practical layer.

The cleanest approach, where both parties are willing and able to coordinate openly, is to treat all household debt as a single combined list for the purposes of the Chapter 3 payoff order, regardless of whose name is on which account — the math behind avalanche, snowball, and the hybrid method doesn't care whose signature is on the original agreement, only about the rate, balance, and available extra payment. This produces the mathematically correct combined order and avoids a common, costly mistake: two people independently running separate, uncoordinated payoff plans on their individual debts, potentially prioritizing a lower-rate individual debt over a higher-rate one carried by the other person, purely because "my debt" and "their debt" got mentally treated as two separate problems rather than one combined one.

Where full coordination isn't practical or desired — separate finances kept deliberately independent within a household, for instance, a legitimate and increasingly common arrangement — each person can still apply this book's frameworks independently and correctly to their own individual debt list; the loss, in that case, is only the marginal optimization available from treating the household as one combined pool, not the correctness of either person's individual plan.

Handling debt during a temporary income gap

A period of unemployment, reduced hours, or an unpaid medical leave changes the calculus across nearly every debt type covered in this chapter, and it's worth addressing directly rather than assuming the standard frameworks apply unmodified during a genuine income gap. The priority order during a temporary gap differs meaningfully from the standard payoff order built in Chapter 3, and it's worth stating explicitly rather than leaving a reader to guess.

During a documented income gap, secured debt (the auto loan, any mortgage) retains its top-priority, non-negotiable status from Chapter 8's framework, for the same reason as always — the consequence of default is losing the asset. Federal student loans move, if anything, further down the urgency list during a genuine income gap, precisely because the income-driven repayment mechanism described earlier in this chapter is built for exactly this scenario — filing for an income-driven recalculation or a deferment, promptly, is usually the correct move the moment a genuine income gap begins, rather than waiting until a payment is actually missed. Unsecured debt — credit cards, personal loans, medical debt — is where the Chapter 4 hardship and negotiation scripts become most valuable during a gap, since issuers and providers generally have far more flexibility to offer a temporary reduced payment or a payment pause for a documented, temporary hardship than they do for an open-ended, unexplained request. The single most important tactical shift during a genuine income gap: call every unsecured creditor proactively, before a payment is missed rather than after, explaining the situation and asking specifically about hardship programs — a proactive call from a still-current account tends to unlock more flexibility than a reactive call made after the account has already gone delinquent.

Private student loans and refinancing: a separate calculation from federal loans

Private student loans, distinct from federal loans throughout this chapter, carry none of the federal protections discussed above regardless of the servicer or lender name on the account, and they should be evaluated using the same rate-based, structurally-honest framework applied to every other unsecured debt in this book. One decision specific to this category worth addressing directly: **refinancing** private student loans into a new private loan, sometimes at a lower rate if credit and income have improved meaningfully since the original loan was taken out (a common scenario for someone several years into a stable career compared to when the loan originated, often as a student or recent graduate with limited credit history).

Refinancing a private loan into a new private loan carries none of the federal-protection-forfeiture risk that makes refinancing a *federal* loan into a private one such a high-stakes decision — since the original loan was already private, there's no protection being given up, only a potential rate improvement to evaluate using the same four-question consolidation test from Chapter 5. The one caution: if a private loan has a creditworthy cosigner (common for loans originated when the borrower was young and had limited independent credit history), refinancing is also an opportunity to evaluate a cosigner release, either through the new loan or, if available, directly through the current servicer — removing a cosigner's ongoing legal obligation is a real, meaningful benefit to that cosigner, independent of any interest-rate improvement, and worth raising explicitly in the refinancing conversation rather than treating the rate as the only variable in play.

A note on for-profit "student loan help" services

Because federal student loan programs and their specific rules shift over time, and because the applications involved (income-driven repayment enrollment, forgiveness program applications) can appear more complicated than they typically are, a real market exists for for-profit companies charging a fee to help borrowers complete the paperwork for these programs. Plainly: every core federal student loan program discussed in this chapter — income-driven repayment enrollment, deferment and forbearance requests, forgiveness program applications — can be accessed directly, at no cost, through the loan servicer or the Department of Education's Federal Student Aid office. A fee-charging service isn't necessarily fraudulent, but it isn't providing access to anything that isn't already available directly and without charge, and that distinction matters before paying anyone a fee to fill out paperwork that's freely available to complete independently.

Chapter 9 — What to Do After Debt-Free

The situation

The last payment clears. The final account shows a zero balance. For most people who've spent a year, two years, five years methodically working through the order built in Chapters 2 and 3, this moment is treated as the finish line — the plan's explicit endpoint, the thing every prior chapter was building toward. It's also, mechanically, the single most common point where the entire structure that got someone to zero starts breaking down, because the plan had a detailed answer for every dollar up to this point and, for a large share of people, no explicit answer at all for what happens the day after.

The mechanics

The debt payoff plan freed up a specific, sizable amount of monthly cash flow — every minimum payment that used to go to now-closed accounts, plus the extra payment amount that had been rolling forward from each cleared debt to the next. In the six- and seven-debt examples used throughout this book, that freed-up amount often runs into several hundred dollars a month, sometimes close to a thousand. That number doesn't disappear when the last debt clears. It has to go somewhere, and if no explicit destination has been decided in advance, it defaults to wherever the path of least resistance happens to lead — which is very often back into discretionary spending, at a pace that can rebuild a meaningful balance within a year or two, on the same accounts that were just paid off.

This isn't a willpower failure or a character flaw. It's the predictable result of a structural gap: months or years of disciplined redirection ending with no plan for what the redirected money does next. A payoff plan that doesn't explicitly answer "what happens to this money on day one after the last payment" is an incomplete plan, regardless of how well it executed everything before that point.

There's a second mechanical risk specific to the immediate post-payoff period: **the absence of an emergency fund**. Many aggressive payoff plans, in the interest of maximizing extra payments, deliberately minimize cash reserves during the payoff period — every spare dollar goes to debt rather than savings. That's often a defensible tradeoff during active payoff, since eliminating a 20%+ interest rate is usually a better return than the near-zero return on a savings account. But it leaves a person freshly debt-free with little to no buffer against the next unplanned expense — a car repair, a medical bill, a period of reduced income — and without a buffer in place, the most likely response to that next unplanned expense is exactly the tool that's now sitting open and available: a credit card. This is the single most common mechanical pathway back into debt after a successful payoff, and it's entirely preventable with an explicit, sequenced plan.

A third factor, stated plainly: **credit score behavior after payoff.** Closing every newly-paid-off account immediately can, in some cases, reduce a credit score in the short term by lowering total available credit (raising utilization on any remaining accounts) and shortening average account age. This doesn't mean accounts should never be closed — there are legitimate reasons to close an account, particularly one with a high annual fee or one that represents a genuine ongoing temptation — but it means the decision should be made deliberately, account by account, rather than either reflexively closing everything the moment it hits zero or reflexively leaving everything open without a management plan.

The framework

A sequenced allocation plan for the freed-up monthly cash flow, to be decided and written down before the last debt payment clears, not after:

Priority one: build or complete a starter emergency fund, commonly recommended in the range of one to three months of essential expenses, before redirecting freed-up cash flow anywhere else. If a starter fund was already built during the payoff period (a reasonable choice for some households, weighed against the interest-rate math in Chapter 1), this step may already be satisfied — verify the balance is still intact and adequate, since a full payoff push sometimes draws down an existing fund.

Priority two: extend the emergency fund toward a fuller reserve (commonly cited in the three-to-six-month range, adjusted for job stability and household circumstances) before redirecting cash flow to discretionary spending increases or long-term investing. This is the buffer that keeps the next unplanned expense from becoming the seed of a new debt cycle.

Priority three: make an explicit decision about every newly-closed-to-zero account — keep open and unused, keep open and used for planned, budgeted spending paid in full monthly, freeze via the issuer's lock feature, or close. Write the decision down for each account, with a reason, rather than leaving it as an unexamined default.

Priority four: only after priorities one through three are addressed, redirect the freed-up monthly amount toward a forward-looking goal — retirement contributions, a house down payment, other savings goals — with the same explicit, written specificity that governed the debt payoff order itself. The habit of tracking a number monthly, built over the course of the payoff plan, transfers directly and usefully to tracking a savings or investment balance instead; the mechanism that sustained the payoff (Chapter 7's visible-progress principle) works identically in reverse, on a balance that's now growing instead of shrinking.

A specific guardrail worth adopting explicitly: a 24-hour waiting period on any new revolving debt for the first twelve months after reaching zero. This isn't a permanent rule, and it isn't a judgment about credit use in general — used deliberately, credit is a normal financial tool. It's a temporary structural safeguard for the specific window when the habits and account balances are most likely to relapse toward their pre-payoff pattern, giving the new post-payoff structure time to become the default rather than the exception.

The worked example

Someone finishes an eighteen-month payoff plan that eliminated $19,000 across four accounts, freeing up $620 a month that had been going to minimums and extra payments combined. Following the sequenced framework: months one through three go entirely to completing a starter emergency fund, since the payoff period had drawn the household's small existing buffer down to almost nothing. Months four through nine extend that fund toward a fuller four-month reserve. During this period, a car repair bill for $840 comes in — paid directly from the emergency fund, in full, with zero new debt incurred, which is the entire point of the sequencing: the fund existed specifically to absorb an event exactly like this one before it could restart the credit card cycle.

At month ten, with the emergency fund complete, the explicit account review happens: two of the four newly-paid-off cards get frozen via the issuer's app (kept for credit-history-length reasons, but made deliberately harder to use impulsively), one with a manageable annual fee and rewards program the household actually uses gets kept open and active, budgeted and paid in full monthly, and one — carrying a fee and no meaningful benefit — gets closed outright. From month ten forward, the full $620 redirects to a retirement contribution increase, tracked with the same monthly visible-number habit that carried the payoff plan itself. Two years after the last debt payment, the accounts remain at zero, the emergency fund remains intact, and the freed-up cash flow has a name and a destination instead of an absence where a plan should have been.

Teaching the system to someone else, even if you don't strictly have to

Once a payoff plan has actually run to completion, a specific opportunity opens up that's easy to overlook amid the relief of reaching zero: the frameworks in this book, having just been proven out against a real, personal set of numbers, are now far more credible and far easier to explain to someone else — a partner, an adult child, a sibling, a close friend — than they would have been as abstract advice from a book neither of you had tested. Explaining the true-cost calculation from Chapter 1, or the avalanche-versus-snowball math from Chapter 2, to someone else using your own actual numbers as the worked example, is one of the more effective ways to cement the mechanics permanently in your own thinking, beyond whatever benefit it provides the person you're explaining it to.

This isn't framed as an obligation — plenty of people reach debt-free status and reasonably prefer to keep the details of their own financial history private, and that's a completely legitimate choice. It's an option worth raising specifically because the act of teaching a mechanical system, out loud, to another real person, is a genuinely different and often deeper form of understanding than having read about it — the kind of understanding that makes the guardrails in this chapter (the account decisions, the emergency fund sequencing, the annual review) feel like second nature rather than a checklist to be consulted, which is exactly the state that makes a genuine, permanent debt-free status most likely to actually hold.

Deciding what "debt-free" actually means for your own plan

Before the sequenced framework in this chapter can be applied, it's worth resolving a definitional question some readers will hit and others won't: does "debt-free" mean every debt of every kind, including a mortgage and any remaining student loans on a manageable, protected repayment plan, or does it mean specifically the higher-rate, unsecured, non-protected debt this book has spent most of its chapters addressing? Both are legitimate definitions, and different households reasonably land on different answers, but the answer should be decided explicitly rather than left ambiguous, because it changes when this chapter's framework actually activates.

Many readers using this book's frameworks are working primarily on credit cards, personal loans, medical debt, and similar higher-rate, unsecured balances, while carrying a mortgage and possibly federal student loans on their own separate, longer-horizon tracks — tracks this book has deliberately treated differently throughout (Chapter 8's segmented approach) precisely because a low-rate, protected, long-term secured debt like a mortgage doesn't behave like the debt this book is built to eliminate aggressively. For a household in this position, it's entirely reasonable to treat "debt-free" as "the aggressive-payoff list from Chapter 3 is at zero" and apply this chapter's full framework at that point, even while a mortgage continues on its normal, separate track for years afterward. The point isn't which definition is correct in some abstract sense — it's that whichever definition you're using should be explicit, so the sequenced plan in this chapter activates at the actual moment it's meant to, rather than being indefinitely deferred while waiting for a mortgage that was never part of the original aggressive-payoff plan to also reach zero.

Specific triggers to watch for in year one

Beyond the general risk of undirected cash flow, a handful of specific, predictable moments tend to be where a fresh debt-free status is most likely to slip, and they deserve naming individually rather than treating "relapse" as one vague, undifferentiated risk.

The first major unplanned expense — not covered in this book's earlier car-repair example only because it's hypothetical, but because it is, statistically, close to universal. Nearly every household encounters some unplanned expense of meaningful size within a given year — a repair, a medical copay, an appliance failure, travel for a family emergency. Whether that expense gets absorbed by an emergency fund or resolved with a new credit card charge is almost entirely a function of whether the fund existed and was adequately sized at the moment the expense arrived, which is precisely why priority one and two in this chapter's framework come before anything else, including further debt payoff momentum or investing.

The first holiday season or major gift-giving period after reaching zero deserves specific, deliberate planning rather than being treated as a normal month. Discretionary spending during these periods tends to run higher than average across a wide range of households, and a debt-free status with no explicit holiday budget set in advance is a common point where a first new balance quietly appears — not from a single large purchase, usually, but from several moderate ones spread across a few weeks, each individually justified, together adding up to a real balance by the following January.

The first "we deserve this" moment — a specific psychological trigger worth naming plainly even in a book that otherwise stays out of psychological territory, because it has a purely tactical fix. After a long, disciplined payoff period, a real and understandable impulse toward a reward — a vacation, a larger purchase, something that marks the achievement — is common and not inherently a problem. The tactical fix isn't to suppress the impulse; it's to fund it deliberately, from the sequenced plan in this chapter (a specific savings line within priority four, rather than an unplanned charge), so the reward exists inside the structure instead of outside it, undermining the very structure that made the payoff possible in the first place.

Building the framework into a written, one-page document

Everything in this chapter's framework works best written down, in a single document, completed before the last debt payment clears rather than assembled reactively afterward. A workable one-page structure: the target emergency fund amount and current progress toward it; an explicit line for each currently-open, newly-paid-off account with its decision (keep open and used, keep open and unused, frozen, or closed) and the reasoning; the freed-up monthly dollar amount and its intended destination once priorities one and two are satisfied; and a specific, named plan for the next major discretionary spending period (holidays, a vacation, a large planned purchase) with a dollar figure attached rather than an open-ended intention. A document like this takes perhaps twenty minutes to build and functions as the single clearest defense against the structural gap this entire chapter describes — the plan that ends at the last payment with nothing written for what comes next.

Lifestyle inflation and the specific version of it that follows a payoff

A related but distinct risk from the ones already covered in this chapter deserves its own direct treatment: lifestyle inflation, in general, refers to spending rising to consume any increase in available income, and a debt payoff produces exactly this kind of income increase in the form of freed-up monthly cash flow, even though no raise or promotion actually occurred. The mechanics of this risk are identical to lifestyle inflation following any income increase, but the debt-payoff-specific version deserves its own direct name, since it's easy to miss precisely because no external event (a new job, a raise) marks the moment the available cash flow changed — the change happens quietly, internally, the moment the final payment clears, with no external signal prompting a deliberate decision about what to do with it.

This is, in effect, the same core problem this chapter's entire framework exists to solve, restated from a different angle: freed-up cash flow that isn't given an explicit destination doesn't sit neutrally waiting for a decision — it tends to get absorbed gradually into a slightly higher baseline of everyday spending, in amounts small enough that no single purchase feels like the moment lifestyle inflation happened, the same way no single missed calculation feels like the moment a minimum-payment debt became expensive back in Chapter 1. The sequenced framework earlier in this chapter — emergency fund, then account decisions, then an explicit forward destination for the remaining freed-up amount — is the direct structural defense against this exact pattern, and it's worth returning to that framework specifically, rather than treating lifestyle inflation as a separate problem requiring a separate solution.

An annual review ritual, once the immediate post-payoff period has passed

The specific triggers and immediate sequencing covered earlier in this chapter address the first twelve to eighteen months after debt-free status. It's worth establishing a lighter-weight, ongoing ritual for the years beyond that window, since the risk of quietly drifting back toward debt doesn't disappear once the first year has passed cleanly — it simply becomes less acute and less closely watched, which is exactly the condition under which a slow drift is most likely to go unnoticed until it's become a real balance again.

A workable annual review, scheduled on a fixed date (a birthday, the anniversary of the final debt payment, the start of a new year — the specific date matters less than its being fixed and recurring rather than "whenever it comes to mind"), covers four questions: is the emergency fund still at its target level, or has it quietly been drawn down for non-emergencies without being replenished; are any of the accounts kept open from the original payoff plan carrying a balance that wasn't paid in full that month, which is the single clearest early sign of drift back toward revolving debt; has the freed-up monthly cash flow's destination (priority four from this chapter's framework) actually been followed, or has it silently been absorbed into general spending without an explicit decision to redirect it; and has any new debt been taken on in the past year, and if so, was it a deliberate, evaluated decision using this book's frameworks, or an unplanned one. A twenty-minute annual check against these four questions catches the kind of gradual, unremarkable drift that a full year of otherwise-normal life can produce without ever feeling, on any single day, like a decision was made to go back into debt.

Rebuilding credit after a payoff period, mechanically

For some readers, the debt eliminated by this book's frameworks includes accounts that went to collections or were settled, and it's worth addressing directly what happens to credit standing during the months and years after a payoff plan concludes, since "pay everything off" and "credit score fully recovered" are not the same event, and treating them as identical produces unrealistic expectations about the recovery timeline.

Credit scoring models generally weigh several factors: payment history (the largest single factor in most common scoring models), amounts owed relative to available credit, length of credit history, mix of credit types, and new credit inquiries. A payoff plan directly improves the "amounts owed" factor immediately and substantially — this is often the fastest-moving component of a credit score, and it's common to see a meaningful score improvement within a few months of eliminating high-utilization revolving balances, well before any of the other factors have had time to shift. Payment history, by contrast, is a longer game: a past late payment or a settled/collections notation remains visible on a credit report for a set period (commonly around seven years for most negative marks, though the exact treatment varies by item type), and its negative weight diminishes gradually over that period rather than disappearing on a fixed date, meaning its practical impact on a specific credit decision (a mortgage application, for instance) tends to shrink well before the seven-year mark, particularly as it's joined by a growing, more recent history of on-time payments.

The single most useful, purely mechanical thing to do during this recovery period, beyond the account-level decisions covered earlier in this chapter, is maintaining low utilization and perfect on-time payment on whatever accounts remain open and active — since payment history and utilization are the two most responsive factors, consistent behavior on these two fronts tends to produce visible improvement faster than the passage of time alone. It's also true that pulling your own credit report — through the free channels available to U.S. consumers for checking their own credit — does not itself affect your score in any way; a "soft" self-inquiry is treated differently than a "hard" inquiry initiated by a lender reviewing a new credit application, and checking your own report periodically during a recovery period is a useful, cost-free way to track real progress and catch any reporting errors early, rather than guessing at how the process is going.

Chapter 10 — The Ten Mistakes That Keep People in Debt Longest

The situation

Every mistake in this chapter shows up repeatedly across debt payoff situations, regardless of income level, debt size, or which method — avalanche, snowball, or hybrid — someone chose to follow. None of them are exotic. All of them are avoidable with the frameworks already covered in this book, which makes them worth gathering in one place as a final, explicit checklist rather than trusting that reading each chapter once was enough to prevent all ten from creeping in individually.

The mechanics and the ten mistakes

Mistake one: paying only the minimum without ever calculating the real cost. Covered in full in Chapter 1 — the minimum payment formula is structurally designed to extend payoff time, and skipping the real-interest-cost calculation is the single most expensive mistake in this entire list, because every other mistake compounds on top of it.

Mistake two: picking a payoff method by feel or by which book was read first, rather than running the actual numbers. Chapter 2 exists because "avalanche versus snowball" is usually presented as an ideological choice when it's actually a calculable one. Skipping the calculation means guessing at a decision that takes fifteen minutes to answer with real numbers.

Mistake three: ignoring the small-balance quick-win adjustment entirely, or over-applying it to every debt regardless of size. Both directions of this error cost real money — pure avalanche with no adjustment risks abandonment on long timelines (Chapter 7); over-applying the small-balance rule to every mid-size debt erodes the avalanche's mathematical advantage far more than the calculated, bounded version in Chapter 3.

Mistake four: never calling to negotiate, on the assumption that rates and balances are fixed. Chapter 4's core message — that meaningful negotiation room often exists on both current accounts and collections accounts — goes unused by a large share of people carrying debt, simply because the option doesn't occur to them as available.

Mistake five: agreeing to a settlement or hardship arrangement over the phone without getting it in writing before paying. This single omission has, in real cases, turned a good-faith negotiated agreement into a dispute with no enforceable record. It's the cheapest possible insurance against a real risk, and it's skipped constantly, usually in the relief of finally reaching a resolution.

Mistake six: consolidating debt without answering what happens to the reopened credit lines. Chapter 5's third mechanical risk — the reopened-line relapse — is not rare. A consolidation loan performing exactly as designed can still coexist with a worse overall financial position if the freed-up cards silently refill without an explicit plan.

Mistake seven: consolidating federal student loans into a private loan without understanding the protections being permanently forfeited. This is the single highest-stakes version of mistake six, covered directly in Chapters 5 and 8, and it's irreversible once done — worth double-checking before signing anything that would convert federal loans into a private consolidation product.

Mistake eight: opening a balance transfer without a concrete plan to clear the balance before the promotional rate expires. Chapter 6's fixed-target rule — dividing the balance by the number of promotional months to set a non-negotiable payment floor — exists specifically because the card's actual minimum payment will never clear the balance in time on its own, and drifting along at that minimum is the most common way a 0% offer turns into a worse rate than the one it replaced.

Mistake nine: treating every dollar type identically across a mixed debt portfolio. Chapter 8 exists because federal student loans, secured debt, medical debt, and revolving credit each carry structural features a pure interest-rate sort doesn't capture. The most costly version of this mistake is aggressively paying down protected federal student loans ahead of unprotected high-rate debt, or letting a secured auto loan payment slip to free up cash for a credit card, both of which trade a genuinely bad tradeoff for a marginally faster-looking number on paper.

Mistake ten: reaching zero with no explicit plan for the freed-up cash flow. Chapter 9's entire argument in one line — a payoff plan that ends at the last payment, with no sequenced plan for what comes next, is an incomplete plan, and it's the single most common reason someone who successfully executes everything in Chapters 1 through 8 still ends up carrying meaningful debt again within a few years.

The framework

Run this as a literal checklist against your own plan, in order, before considering it finished:

1. Have I calculated the real total-interest cost of every debt I carry, not just looked at the minimum payment? 2. Have I run both the avalanche and snowball simulations on my actual numbers, and do I know the real dollar gap between them? 3. Have I applied the small-balance quick-win threshold deliberately and with a bounded rule, not randomly or excessively? 4. Have I called or written to every creditor and collector to ask about a rate reduction, hardship program, or

settlement, rather than assuming the stated terms are fixed? 5. Do I have every negotiated agreement in writing, dated, before any payment is sent? 6. If I've consolidated any debt, have I written down an explicit plan for every reopened credit line? 7. Have I confirmed whether any debt I'm consolidating or paying off aggressively is a federal student loan, and adjusted the plan if so? 8. If I have an open balance transfer, do I have a fixed, non-negotiable monthly target calculated to clear it before the promotional period ends? 9. Have I segmented my debts by type (federal student loan, secured, medical, unsecured revolving) and applied the right treatment to each, rather than one blanket rate sort? 10. Do I have a written, sequenced plan for the freed-up cash flow the moment my last debt clears — emergency fund, account decisions, and a forward destination — rather than leaving it to be decided in the moment?

The worked example

A final gut-check, applied to the six-debt, $34,000 example from Chapter 7. Running the checklist: real interest cost calculated on all six debts (yes, mistake one avoided). Avalanche versus hybrid simulation run and the $340 gap known explicitly (yes, mistake two avoided). Small-balance rule applied to exactly one debt meeting the bounded threshold, not several (yes, mistake three avoided). No negotiation attempted yet on the two credit cards in the mix (mistake four still open — a real, actionable next step, not a hypothetical one). No consolidation or balance transfer involved in this particular portfolio (mistakes five, six, seven, and eight not applicable here). Student loan and auto loan treated per Chapter 8's segmented framework rather than a blanket rate sort (mistake nine avoided). No explicit post-payoff plan written yet, since the plan is still eighteen months from completion (mistake ten flagged as a task for month sixteen or seventeen, not month one, but explicitly on the calendar rather than left to chance).

Nine of ten already addressed, one flagged as open with an explicit action attached, one deliberately deferred to the correct future point in the timeline rather than ignored. That's what a genuinely complete plan looks like in practice — not zero remaining gaps, but zero unexamined ones.

A quick-reference summary of every framework in this book

For a reader who's finished all ten chapters and wants a single, condensed reference before applying everything at once, here's every core framework from this book gathered in one place. Chapter 1: calculate real total-interest cost using balance, APR, and payment amount before assuming a minimum payment is manageable. Chapter 2: run both an avalanche and a snowball simulation on your real debts and know the actual dollar gap between them. Chapter 3: sort by rate, exempt true 0% debts, and pull any near-term small balance to the front under a deliberately chosen threshold. Chapter 4: negotiate directly with creditors and collectors using the rate-reduction and settlement scripts, and get every agreement in writing before paying. Chapter 5: run the four-question test on any consolidation offer, with particular caution around federal student loans and reopened credit lines. Chapter 6: calculate the real break-even on any balance transfer and set a fixed, non-negotiable target payment to clear it within the promotional window. Chapter 7: assess your own realistic risk of abandoning a long, low-feedback plan honestly, and weight your payoff order accordingly. Chapter 8: segment mixed debt types — federal student loans, secured debt, medical debt, and unsecured revolving debt — and apply the right treatment to each rather than one blanket rate sort. Chapter 9: build an explicit, sequenced plan for freed-up cash flow before the last debt payment clears, not after. Chapter 10: run the ten-item mistake checklist against your own plan, honestly, before considering it finished.

Ten frameworks, each independently useful, each designed to be run with your own real numbers rather than taken on faith. Together, they're the entire mechanical system this book set out to hand you in the introduction — nothing more mysterious than that, and nothing less complete either.

None of these ten frameworks require the others in order to work. A reader who only ever uses Chapter 4's negotiation scripts, without touching the avalanche-versus-snowball math from Chapter 2, still walks away with real, calculable savings on whatever gets negotiated. A reader who builds the exact payoff order from Chapter 3 but never negotiates a single account still finishes faster and cheaper than a minimum-payment default would have produced on its own. They compound when used together, which is why this book presents them as one connected system rather than ten unrelated tips — but each one stands on its own, which means there's no wrong place to start applying what you've just read, and no requirement to have all ten running at once before any of them starts paying off.

The real cost of doing nothing, stated one final time in full

It's worth closing this chapter, and the tactical portion of this book, with the number every other chapter has been implicitly working against: the cost of continuing to pay minimums with no order, no negotiation, and no explicit plan at all — the default state this entire book exists to move a reader away from. Return to Chapter 1's original example: a $6,000 balance at 22% APR, minimum payments only, over fifteen years, total interest exceeding the original balance. Multiply that pattern across a typical multi-debt portfolio of the kind used throughout this book's worked examples, and the real, uncalculated cost of never applying any of the preceding ten chapters' frameworks routinely runs into five figures over the life of a debt load that could, with the order and tools in this book, have been resolved in a fraction of the time for a fraction of the cost.

That gap — between the default, no-plan outcome and the outcome this book's frameworks produce when actually applied — is the entire value proposition of everything covered so far, stated plainly rather than left implicit. It was never a claim that any individual chapter's specific technique is dramatic or clever on its own. Negotiating a rate reduction, running an avalanche simulation, checking a consolidation offer's total cost before signing — none of these are complicated maneuvers. Their value comes entirely from being applied consistently, in the right order, against real numbers, rather than skipped in favor of the default path of least resistance that a minimum-payment box on a monthly statement quietly, persistently invites.

The single mistake underneath most of the other ten

If the ten mistakes in this chapter share a common root, it's this: treating a debt payoff plan as a one-time decision rather than a system that needs periodic, deliberate maintenance. Every one of the ten items above is, at bottom, a version of the same failure — setting a plan in motion and then either never checking it against reality again (mistakes one, two, and three), never using a tool that requires an active, ongoing choice to engage with rather than a passive default (mistakes four through eight), applying a static framework to a portfolio that actually contains structurally different debt types (mistake nine), or stopping the system entirely the moment its most visible goal is achieved (mistake ten).

The corrective, stated as plainly as the rest of this book: build the plan once, using the real frameworks in Chapters 1 through 9, and then revisit it on a fixed, deliberate cadence — monthly for the basic tracking numbers described in this chapter's final section, and at defined trigger points (a rate change, a windfall, a new debt, a completed payoff) for the larger structural decisions. A plan that gets built once and then genuinely maintained on this kind of cadence will avoid essentially all ten mistakes on this list, not because the person running it is unusually disciplined, but because the maintenance schedule itself is what catches each mistake before it has time to compound into something costly.

Two additional mistakes, less common but costly when they occur

Applying a windfall to the wrong debt without re-checking the order. A tax refund, a bonus, an inheritance, or any other lump sum is, mechanically, best applied using the same order built in Chapter 3 — to whichever debt currently sits first in the sequence — rather than to whichever debt feels most urgent emotionally (often the largest balance, regardless of rate) or whichever debt happens to be top of mind because a statement just arrived. A windfall applied to the wrong debt doesn't just fail to optimize interest savings; because a large payment can change which debts qualify for the small-balance quick-win threshold from Chapter 3, it's worth re-running that check specifically after any lump-sum payment, not just applying the windfall on autopilot to whatever debt was originally first in line.

Treating a single missed or late payment as a reason to abandon the plan entirely. A missed payment happens, particularly across a payoff plan that runs a year or more — an account gets overlooked during a busy month, an autopay fails silently, a payment date gets mentally miscounted. The costly version of this mistake isn't the missed payment itself, which is usually recoverable with a call to the creditor (many issuers will waive a first late fee for an otherwise good-standing account, on request) — it's the psychological spiral that sometimes follows, where a single missed payment gets treated as evidence the whole plan has failed, leading to genuinely abandoning the extra-payment habit for months rather than simply correcting course the following month. A missed payment is a data point, not a verdict. The correct response is identical to the correct response to any other deviation covered in this book: assess it plainly, fix what's fixable, and continue the plan from wherever it currently stands.

Applying the checklist retroactively, mid-plan, not just before starting

Everything in this chapter's ten-item checklist has been framed, throughout the book, as something to verify before or while building a payoff plan. It's equally valuable applied retroactively, at any point mid-plan, especially for a reader who started paying down debt before encountering this book's specific frameworks and is now looking to correct course rather than start from zero. There's no penalty, mechanically, for adopting the avalanche or hybrid order six months into a plan that started as a less-optimized approach — the math simply picks up from whatever the current balances and rates actually are, on the day the corrected order gets applied, and runs forward from there exactly as it would have from day one.

The same applies to negotiation: there's no rule requiring a negotiation attempt to happen at the start of a payoff journey rather than partway through it — a call to a creditor made in month eight of a payoff plan is exactly as valid, and captures exactly as much of the available benefit, as one made in month one. The only genuine cost to adopting this book's frameworks partway through an existing plan, rather than from the very beginning, is the interest that accrued during the months before the correction — a real, non-recoverable cost, but a bounded one, and one that ends the moment the corrected approach actually gets applied. This is worth stating plainly for any reader who started this book already partway into a debt payoff effort: the frameworks in this chapter's checklist, and throughout this book, are just as usable starting today as they would have been starting from a completely fresh slate.

A final mistake, distinct enough to stand on its own: comparing your timeline to someone else's

This mistake doesn't fit neatly into the ten mechanical items above, because it isn't mechanical — it's a comparison error, and it deserves naming directly because it quietly undermines otherwise sound plans often enough to matter. Payoff timelines that circulate publicly — a friend's account of paying off $40,000 in eighteen months, a story shared online about an aggressive multi-year payoff — describe a specific combination of income, expenses, debt size, and interest rates that is very unlikely to match your own combination exactly. A timeline built correctly using this book's frameworks, on your own real numbers, is the right timeline for your situation regardless of whether it's faster or slower than someone else's story, and treating a faster external example as the standard your own plan should have hit is a comparison that produces discouragement without producing any actual improvement to your plan's underlying mechanics.

The corrective isn't to avoid hearing about other people's payoff timelines — they can be genuinely useful for morale and for picking up tactical ideas. It's to keep the comparison at the level of tactics (did they use a negotiation script worth trying, did they find a consolidation structure worth evaluating) rather than at the level of the finish date itself, which is a function of variables specific to their situation and largely irrelevant to whether your own plan, correctly built, is working as designed.

How to know your plan is actually working, independent of how it feels

Because a payoff plan can feel slow even while it's working exactly as designed — particularly in the early months of a pure avalanche order on a large high-rate debt, before Chapter 7's early-win logic has produced a visible milestone — it's worth having an objective check, separate from how the plan feels on a given week, for whether it's actually on track. Two numbers, tracked monthly, answer this reliably: total debt remaining (the same combined number from Chapter 7's tracking recommendation) and, separately, total minimum-payment obligation across all remaining accounts. A total-debt-remaining number that's declining month over month, even slowly, and a total-minimum-payment number that's also declining as accounts close and roll into the next target, are both objective, unambiguous signals that the mechanics are functioning correctly — regardless of whether the process currently feels fast, slow, exciting, or tedious. Trust those two numbers over how any given week feels; the numbers are measuring the actual mechanism this whole book is built around, and the feeling is measuring something else entirely, useful in its own right (Chapter 7 covers exactly why) but not a reliable substitute for the two numbers that actually tell you whether the plan is on track.

Closing

Go back to the number this book opened with: two people, same total debt, same income, same monthly payment, years apart in how long it takes them to reach zero and thousands of dollars apart in what it costs them to get there — for no reason except the order they chose and whether they used the tools available to them along the way. That gap was never about willpower, and it was never really about how much debt either of them started with. It was about mechanics: the sequence, the negotiated terms, the fee math on a consolidation or a transfer, the explicit plan for the freed-up cash flow at the end. Every one of those is a decision you can make correctly with the frameworks in this book, on your own numbers, without needing anyone's permission or anyone else's story about how they finally "got serious about money."

Every chapter in this book has tried to keep one promise: no claim without a calculation behind it, and no calculation without a real, worked number showing exactly how it plays out. That promise is the whole reason this book exists in the form it does — ten chapters, each following the same situation-mechanics-framework-example shape, rather than a single sweeping argument asking for your trust. Trust wasn't really the currency this book was built to trade in. Verifiable math was.

If there's one idea worth carrying forward past the final page, it's this: debt is not a referendum on who you are. It's a financial position with a knowable structure, and knowable structures respond to mechanics, not to sentiment. You don't need to feel different about money to execute the order in Chapter 3 correctly. You don't need to have resolved whatever led to the balance in the first place before you're allowed to start paying it down in the smartest available sequence. The math works the same regardless of how you feel about it on any given Tuesday, which is, in its own way, the most encouraging fact in this entire book — because it means the plan doesn't depend on you having a good day. It only depends on you running the numbers and following the order.

Go get your real numbers, if you haven't already pulled them while reading. Every balance, every rate, every minimum payment. Sort them the way Chapter 3 describes. Make the calls

Chapter 4 describes. Run the tests in Chapters 5 and 6 before signing anything that promises to make this simpler. And when the last balance hits zero, don't close the book there — turn to Chapter 9 and follow the plan for what comes after, because that's the chapter that decides whether this is the last time you ever have to read a book like this one.

A last practical thought, worth carrying forward past this specific debt payoff, whenever it finishes. Every mechanism in this book — the real cost calculation in Chapter 1, the avalanche and hybrid math in Chapters 2 and 3, the negotiation leverage in Chapter 4, the honest evaluation tests in Chapters 5 and 6 — is a general-purpose tool, not a one-time-use instrument specific to the debt you happen to be carrying today. The same true-cost calculation applies to any future loan you consider taking on. The same four-question test applies to any future consolidation or refinancing offer that lands in your inbox years from now. The same negotiation scripts work on a bill that hasn't been issued yet. You're not just paying off a specific set of balances by working through this book — you're building a permanent, reusable set of mechanics for evaluating any future debt decision correctly, the first time, rather than needing to relearn the lesson after a costly one.

That's worth something independent of the current payoff plan's outcome. Debt, in some form, touches nearly every financial life at some point — a future car purchase, a home, an unexpected expense that outpaces available savings. The specific balances in front of you right now will eventually be gone, one way or another. The mechanics in this book don't expire when they are.

There's one more thing worth saying plainly, because it's easy to lose sight of across ten chapters of math, scripts, and frameworks: the number on your final zero-balance statement is not a verdict on who you are, and it was never going to be. It's the closing entry on a specific financial position, resolved with specific, learnable mechanics — the same mechanics available to anyone who picks up this exact book and runs the exact numbers. You picked it up. That's the only qualification the process required.

The order is the whole game. Now go run it.

Notes & Further Reading

The following sources and concepts referenced throughout this book are real, attributed, and independently verifiable — verify current terms, rates, and program details directly with the relevant institution or agency before acting, since consumer credit programs and specific figures change over time.

On the psychological research behind payoff-order behavior: Gal, D., & McShane, B. B. (2012). "Can Small Victories Help Win the War? Evidence from Consumer Debt Management." *Journal of Marketing Research*, 49(4), 487–501. This is the empirical study referenced in Chapter 7, using data from a debt settlement firm to examine the relationship between closing accounts (regardless of balance size) and overall debt elimination outcomes.

On mental accounting and how people treat money non-fungibly: Thaler, R. H. (1999). "Mental Accounting Matters." *Journal of Behavioral Decision Making*, 12(3), 183–206. Thaler, a Nobel laureate in economics, developed the mental accounting framework referenced in this book's broader discussion of how debt and payments get psychologically categorized differently from their actual dollar value.

On present bias and the tendency to discount future costs relative to immediate relief: Laibson, D. (1997). "Golden Eggs and Hyperbolic Discounting." *The Quarterly Journal of Economics*, 112(2), 443–478. This is the foundational academic treatment of hyperbolic discounting, a well-established behavioral-economics concept relevant to why lower minimum payments feel more attractive than their long-run cost would justify.

On debt collection rights: The Fair Debt Collection Practices Act (FDCPA), enforced by the Consumer Financial Protection Bureau (CFPB) and the Federal Trade Commission (FTC), governs permissible debt collection practices in the United States, including debt validation rights and communication restrictions referenced in Chapter 4. Current guidance and complaint filing are available directly through the CFPB's consumer resources.

On debt settlement industry practices and consumer warnings: The Federal Trade Commission's Telemarketing Sales Rule, amended in 2010 to specifically regulate for-profit debt relief and settlement services, and the FTC's own published consumer guidance on debt settlement, are the relevant regulatory sources for anyone considering a third-party debt settlement company rather than direct creditor negotiation as described in Chapter 4.

On nonprofit credit counseling resources: The National Foundation for Credit Counseling (NFCC) is a real, established nonprofit umbrella organization accrediting member credit counseling agencies across the United States, offering free or low-cost budget and debt counseling as an alternative or supplement to the self-directed frameworks in this book.

On the debt snowball as a popularized (non-academic) practitioner method: the smallest-balance-first approach discussed throughout this book, particularly in Chapters 2, 3, and 7, has been widely popularized in personal finance media under the "debt snowball" name; it is a practitioner-originated term rather than an academic one, distinct from — but consistent with the direction of — the Gal and McShane (2012) findings cited above.

On federal student loan repayment and protections: current details on income-driven repayment plans, deferment, forbearance, and forgiveness programs referenced in Chapter 8 are maintained directly by the U.S. Department of Education's Federal Student Aid office and should be verified there directly, given how frequently program terms and eligibility criteria are updated.

On the Truth in Lending Act (TILA): this federal law, enforced in coordination between the Federal Reserve, the CFPB, and other regulators depending on the institution type, requires lenders to disclose the Annual Percentage Rate and other standardized cost terms on consumer credit products, referenced in Chapter 1's discussion of what APR discloses and what it doesn't fully capture (such as compounding frequency and certain fee structures).

On the Fair Credit Reporting Act (FCRA): this federal law governs how long negative items may remain on a consumer credit report (generally around seven years for most derogatory marks, longer for certain bankruptcy filings), consumers' right to dispute inaccurate information, and the requirement behind the official, federally mandated free annual credit report access point (operated jointly by the three major credit bureaus — Equifax, Experian, and TransUnion — under FCRA requirements), referenced in Chapter 9's discussion of credit recovery timelines and self-inquiry.

On general credit scoring factors: the broad categories of factors used in most widely adopted U.S. credit scoring models (payment history, amounts owed, length of credit history, credit mix, and new credit) are publicly documented by FICO and VantageScore, the two most widely used scoring model providers, and are the basis for the general, model-agnostic discussion of scoring behavior in Chapters 5 and 9 — specific score-point impacts vary by model version and individual credit profile and were deliberately not quoted as fixed numbers in this book for that reason.

A general note on this book's approach to sourcing: every specific dollar figure, percentage, and worked-example number throughout the preceding ten chapters is illustrative, chosen to demonstrate a calculation clearly, and is not a claim about any particular lender's current rates or any specific real account. Every named concept, law, or piece of research above, by contrast, is real, independently verifiable, and cited as precisely as this book's format allows. Where a claim could not be verified with confidence, it was either cut or explicitly framed as a general convention or author framework rather than a sourced fact — that distinction is maintained deliberately throughout this book, and it's worth applying the same standard to anything else you read on this subject.

About the Author

Daniel Cross writes the Wealth Mechanics series, a set of tactical, mechanics-first guides to specific money decisions — negotiation, debt payoff, pricing, and the practical systems behind building financial stability. Each book in the series is built around the same principle: real leverage, real math, and concrete, reusable frameworks, rather than motivational reframing or a personality diagnosis. Daniel's background is in consumer lending and credit underwriting, where the frameworks in this book were first tested against real accounts, real negotiations, and real payoff timelines before ever being written down.

The Wealth Mechanics series is built on a simple premise: money decisions are made easier not by feeling more confident about them, but by understanding the actual mechanics underneath them clearly enough to act without hesitation. Each volume takes one specific, high-stakes financial decision — a negotiation, a debt payoff, a pricing structure, an automated savings system — and breaks it down into the exact, reusable steps a reader can apply immediately, using their own real numbers, without needing to trust the author's judgment over their own once the mechanics have been explained. Future volumes in the series continue applying that same standard to other specific, high-leverage money decisions most people are never taught to approach systematically.

Also in the Series

Every book in Wealth Mechanics stands on its own — read them in any order. If this one was useful, the library continues:

The Negotiation Playbook

The Pricing Playbook

The Automatic Wealth System

The Savings Rate Playbook

The Investment Onboarding Playbook

The Side Income Playbook

The Real Estate Entry Playbook

The Tax Reduction Playbook

The Equity Compensation Playbook

www.ingramcontent.com/pod-product-compliance
Lightning Source LLC
LaVergne TN
LVHW010719061126
851857LV00014B/1262
* 9 7 8 1 8 0 4 2 8 1 1 9 2 *